MANAGING
UP,
MANAGING
DOWN

How to Be a
Better Manager
and Get What You Want
from Your Boss
and Your Staff

MANAGING UP, MANAGING DOWN

by Mary Ann Allison
and Eric W. Allison

Illustrations by Thomas L. Hecht

Cornerstone Library
Published by Simon & Schuster, Inc.
NEW YORK

Published by Cornerstone Library
A Division of Simon & Schuster, Inc.
Simon & Schuster Building
Rockefeller Center
1230 Avenue of the Americas
New York, New York 10020

CORNERSTONE LIBRARY and colophon are registered
trademarks of Simon & Schuster, Inc.
10 9 8 7 6 5 4 3 2 1
Manufactured in the United States of America

Library of Congress Cataloging in Publication Data
Allison, Mary Ann.
   Managing up, managing down.
   1. Personnel management. 2. Organizational behavior. 3.
Psychology, Industrial. I. Allison, Eric W. (Eric William) II. Title.
HF5549.A559   1984   658.4   83-27214
ISBN: 0-346-12639-8

To Ann Wiseman, who asked for this book;
Linda Lash, who provided so many examples;
Barbara Gess, who made it better;
and
To those who led and those who followed us—with thanks

CONTENTS

SECTION II
MANAGING DOWN

SECTION III
MANAGING LATERALLY

PREFACE

Why another book on management when there are so many already available? What makes this book different?

Most books on management fall into one of two categories. One is general and theoretical and is an excellent guide to the proper way to run a large corporation. The second is oriented toward specifics, for example, power, clothes, or understanding data processing. Both kinds of books have a place on the manager's bookshelf, but neither answers the questions of most new, aspiring, or current middle managers.

Middle management is make-or-break time for a career. Getting into the bottom rungs of middle management, in fact, can mean you *have* a career rather than a job. The range of positions that fit into the general category of middle management is so vast that a very successful and remunerative career can be carved out without ever reaching senior management—if you do those tasks well. If your goal is senior management, your mid-level performance will determine whether or not you ever get a chance at it.

This book is designed to help you succeed in the business world by succeeding as a middle manager. Whether you are a middle manager or hope to be one, this book will help you achieve that success. Usually, you have to learn the techniques presented here by trial and error or by watching a successful manager and figuring out what he or she is doing right. If you are lucky, mentors might be able to teach you some of these techniques—but only if they are truly aware of how or why they do what they do.

Whether your job is accounting, purchasing, editing, service, or production, middle management always involves dealing with people in order to get the work done. This book will not tell you how to budget, forecast, design, or prepare PERT charts. It will tell you how to work with and manage people.

People—superiors, subordinates, and peers—can be at once the most difficult and the most rewarding part of the job. No matter how good you are personally, promotion and salary increases come to a middle manager only through the accomplishment of tasks that require a team effort. *Your* success will depend on your staff and on your boss. This book tells you how to *manage* both. Finally, by concentrating on the people element of the management task, this book is also designed to make your job more fulfilling.

The contents are practical rather than theoretical, with real examples taken from many different types of management situations. Charts, diagrams, and personal check-lists are included to make the transfer of skills to the job easier.

"But I am working hard, dear. . . ."

Find someplace comfortable—the beach or your backyard or a good chair in front of a fire—to read these chapters. When you are finished, put the book in the bottom drawer of your desk at work for reference. Good luck. Managing is hard but rewarding work.

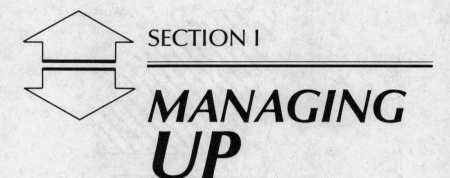

SECTION I

MANAGING UP

Introduction

*E*xecutives work long hours. If you're a middle manager now, you already know that. If you want to be one, it's a fact of life you should learn. Don't be fooled by the myth that the higher you go in a company, the less you have to work. It just isn't true, and if your reason for wanting promotion is so you can relax, you might as well learn the truth now and avoid disappointment.

A middle manager spends an average of 45 to 50 hours at work each week—and many work even more. It is one of the differences between a salaried manager and an hourly wage supervisor. A wage earner goes home when it's "quitting time." A manager leaves when the work is done—or takes it home.

Fifty hours is about 30 percent of the hours in a week. Let's take the computation a little farther. That same manager probably sleeps about 56 hours a week. Deduct sleeping time from the equation and suddenly the time spent at work is about 45 percent of time awake. And that's not counting commutation time, weekend meetings, and business trips.

CHART 1.1

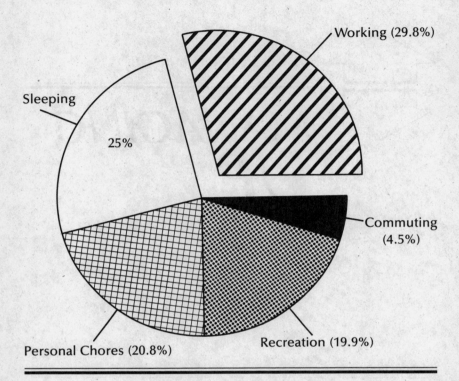

WEEKLY TIME USE

Working (29.8%)

Sleeping

25%

Commuting (4.5%)

Personal Chores (20.8%)

Recreation (19.9%)

What this means is that you probably spend more time at work than you spend with friends, with your spouse or children, or on recreation. The conditions of your job are a major part of your life—and the person, beside yourself, who has the greatest influence on your working life is your boss.

Think about it. More of your waking life may be affected by your boss than by anyone else.

Sound scary? That's why you need to know how to manage up.

Just as a successful marriage is the product of hard work and planning, a successful relationship with your boss also requires forethought and prepa- ration. Your boss directly affects your income, your status, and the greater part of your working life. What happens to you at work has a positive or negative effect on your life away from work. Your salary has an affect on most aspects of your life-style; other factors, such as stress, can have major consequences in your life. Status—title and position—can be nearly as important away from work as it is at work.

It follows that in addition to mastering the technical aspects of a middle-management position the middle manager should try to exercise some control over the work environment. Managing your staff and working with your peers will be covered later. This section of the book deals with how to manage your boss.

Managing your boss may sound contradictory, but it isn't. The next chapter includes the techniques for getting support for your ideas, the proper way to ask for a raise or a promotion, and the right way to say no. It describes how to provide staff support in such a way as to highlight *your* strengths and how to find and work with mentors and godfathers. It shows how to avoid the pitfalls of office politics. Most importantly, it tells you how to get what you want from your boss for your mutual advantage.

1

You and
Your Boss

PART I:

Figuring Out
Where You Are

Your boss is the most critical person in your career. Whether you're fired, left alone, or promoted is dependent on your boss's judgment. Therefore, time invested in working with your boss is a good investment in your career.

Let's begin with an example that illustrates the problems of a bad working relationship.

From Hero to Turkey in Three Short Weeks

Alan was a middle manager, having worked his way up through the ranks at Amalgamated Manhole. He and his wife, Rosemarie, were proud of his accomplishments. He did his job well and confidently expected to be promoted at his next review. Then his manager was transferred to the Fireplug division and a new manager moved in as his boss. Almost immediately, things seemed to go downhill.

The new manager found fault with everything Alan did. Reports that would have pleased his old manager were returned as unsatisfactory. He was criticized for wasting too much of his new boss's time on details, yet castigated for not keeping the new manager informed. His work load multiplied as he continually redid reports and projects. Alan couldn't figure out what he was doing wrong.

His performance hadn't changed, he was sure of that; in fact, he thought he was actually doing better. He had met all goals before they were due and even reduced expenses by 10 percent.

Yet Alan felt uncomfortable all the time. His sense of security was gone. Far from looking forward to a promotion, he now suffered from the nagging fear that he might be fired some Friday afternoon. The situation at work was beginning to affect his personal life. He was short-tempered, snapping at his wife. Worse, several times during the past week he arrived home hours later than he had promised. Rosemarie didn't mind an occasional late night when it was planned, but when he had to stay without warning—and, especially, when he was too late for his daughter's birthday party—it was too much.

Alan couldn't understand it: he had apparently gone from being a rising star to being a turkey within three weeks. It seemed incredible that such a huge change could take place in such a short time.

Alan's problem is one of the most difficult for a manager—or anyone—to face. He had not changed his behavior. Nothing that *Alan* had done had caused a sudden change in his performance. Rather, the

change had been outside of Alan's control—*and he had failed to adapt to it.*

A major factor in Alan's environment had changed: *his manager.* Alan was, of course, perfectly aware that he had a new boss, but he had continued to operate in the manner that had been considered acceptable—in fact, praiseworthy—by his old manager. He listened to his new boss and complied with what he thought he heard. When what Alan considered a perfectly satisfactory report was returned to him for rewriting, he tried to make it better—more of the same—without considering that perhaps what was needed was for him to do it *differently.*

Every manager (including Alan in his relationships with *his* own subordinates) has certain ways he or she wants things done. Some of these may be idiosyncratic or dictated by events the subordinates know nothing about. If a new boss fails to explain the changes adequately—or if Alan, accustomed to his old manager's ways, fails to understand what is being discussed—it behooves Alan to investigate until he does understand. Otherwise, as long as he is merely trying to improve instead of change his work, Alan will continue to fail in the new boss's eyes.

Because Alan failed to take this into consideration, he was miserable personally and his career was suffering—even though his performance had not changed. The change of environment—and his failure to adapt to it—was nullifying Alan's hard work and obscuring his potential.

Fortunately, there is a way to prevent this scenario.

Analyzing Your Situation—Where Are You Now?

Whether you are dealing with a business plan or a personal relationship, you would not expect it to succeed without careful thought. The success of your own career can be greatly aided by an investigation of your own and your manager's environment.

First analyze yourself within your professional environment.

● What responsibilities do you have? (Are you line operations or staff—or a mixture of both? Do you have bottom-line responsibility? How important to the overall business objectives is your area?)

● How well are you supported on the job by your staff? (Do you have to monitor your staff all the time? If you go on vacation, does the work continue? Can they do their own jobs, or are you spending much of your day in hand-holding and training?)

- What other areas within the organization are vital to the completion of your work? (Can you accomplish your assignments without the cooperation of other departments? Do those other areas share a reporting line or are they totally independent? Will they help or hinder you?)

- Are you new on the job or an old timer? (Do you know the company's official policies *and* unspoken procedures? Do you know the people who can shortcut red tape for you? Are you aware of power centers? Do you know who you can safely ignore and who you can't? Do you really know *your* job or are you still learning it?)

- Do you have a nice office or a desk in the hall? (What kind of standing do you have in the office power structure? Is your office on executive row or in the local equivalent of Siberia? Do your subordinates think you are important? Do your peers? People in other departments?)

- Is the political atmosphere supportive? (Will other departments give you the help you may need? What kind of priority do you have? If you need a bigger budget can you get one? Are you likely to step on anyone's toes if you succeed? If you don't?)

- What aspirations do you have? (Are you happy where you are or do you want to move up? How hard are you willing to work to make yourself look good? What are you best at? Do you want to stay in the department/division/area where you are now if you are promoted, or do you want to move on? Would you be willing to relocate? Do you *want* to relocate?)

Take some time to really think through your work life. Don't stop with these questions. If you can think of others, answer them as well. The strategy you follow will depend in large measure on your responses.

For instance, it is not uncommon for executives to work extremely hard, even overwork, until they reach a certain level—manager, perhaps, or vice president—and then decide not to work as hard. This does not necessarily mean such people become inefficient or unambitious; it may simply mean that they will no longer sacrifice everything for their jobs. They often continue to perform well and will probably be promoted, but not as fast. But when executives decide to stop working as hard, they must lower their expectations as well. A sudden—or even gradual—change in work habits can also change a manager's relationship with the boss. The key is often not *what* you do but an awareness that you are doing it—and the *managing* of the changed environment.

Picture the ideal job for you: only you can decide what it is. Define it clearly and remember it often. Then you will be able to work towards it.

Walk a Mile in Your Boss's Shoes

After you have a complete picture of yourself, look at your boss from the same perspective. Ask the same questions about your manager that you asked about yourself, changing the angle a little:

- What is his or her environment?
- What does he or she expect in the way of staff support?
- What support is actually received?
- What is your manager's next career step?
- How well does your manager's boss like him or her?

Walk in your manager's shoes long enough to get a good sense of the surroundings. Be careful not to pass over this too lightly. A superficial study will be more likely to mislead than to help. Chart 1.2 gives you some good ways to start.

CHART 1.2

LEARNING MORE ABOUT YOUR BOSS

1. **LISTEN**   Listen to *what* your boss says, *how* it is said, and what reasoning is offered.

2. **READ**   Read your boss's memos and reports. How does your boss write to his or her boss? Peers? Staff?

3. **WATCH**   Watch your boss in meetings and working with others. With whom does your boss spend time? Why?

4. **ASK**   Ask people who have worked for your boss before how they perceived your boss as a manager.

You cannot manage your boss if you don't understand the job your boss is expected to do. This does not mean that *you* can do his job, but it does mean that you have some grasp of what performance is expected of your manager by senior management. That expectation has a direct effect on you, for the work you do for your manager is a part of the work your manager is expected to accomplish for his or her superiors.

You might think some of the questions above are frivolous. They're not. Consider the question of physical environment. Does your boss have an office commensurate with his or her title? If not, why not? Is it a matter of budget problems? Is the space the department is allocated too small? Is your manager the junior person among his or her peers? Is your manager's department politically feeble?

Any of these reasons could have a profound effect on your boss and, as a result, on you. You may have to produce work superior to the company norm because your boss—or your boss's boss—is trying to overcome handicaps barely visible at your level. To succeed you either produce at that level or transfer to a different department.

But that transfer might take you off a fast track. If you haven't analyzed the environment, you have no way of knowing.

Analyzing Personal Factors

After you have studied the environment, it is time to look at the way you and your boss relate. Alan knew that he and his manager rubbed each other the wrong way, but he failed to perceive the situation as a managerial problem.

Consider this problem as you would a sudden drop in productivity. Begin by assessing potential causes. Take a personal inventory of yourself and your boss. Chart 1.3, "Establishing a Working Relationship, Personal Factors" will help you do this.

The chart is a comparative one. Write down, in however much detail you feel you need, the important things about yourself in each category, then contrast them with the characteristics you see in your boss. The areas of conflict will become readily apparent.

If you consider yourself a "morning person" and your manager "not a morning person," take note. You may be bright and cheery in the morning, but if you disturb your manager with questions and reports while he or she is still struggling to wake up, your career is going to

CHART 1.3

ESTABLISHING A WORKING RELATIONSHIP
PERSONAL FACTORS

Trait	You	Your Manager	Match?	Action Needed?
Age				
Race				
Sex				
Background				
Preferred method of communication (in person, memo . . .)				
Frequency of communication				
Level of detail (to be managed personally)				
Style of dress				
Prejudices				
Sense of humor				
Willingness to take risks				
Acceptance of change				
Preferred personal presentation style				
Time of day				

suffer. Conversely, if your manager likes to start work early and you can't think before 10 A.M., you have a problem. You may appear dull and stupid simply because you aren't awake yet. The solution may be to get up earlier and go jogging.

Here's an example:

Trait	You	Your Manager	Match?	Action Needed?
Age	27	59	No	

If your section on age looks like this—or exactly the reverse—you may be intimidating to your manager. Be careful. Although intimidation of your superior may work in the short term, in the long term most managers will retaliate. Here's one solution:

Trait	You	Your Manager	Match?	Action Needed?
Age	27	59	No	• Understand she may feel I'm too young. • Talk less about winning at racketball.

This doesn't mean people of different ages can't work together harmoniously, nor is it a recommendation to practice discrimination. Nevertheless, in the real world people aren't perfect, and differences in temperament, age, sex, rigidity of mind or willingness to take risks can be sources of friction. Awareness of this potential takes you a long way toward preventing these differences from interfering with your working relationships. In a good business environment those same differences can contribute to a diversity of outlook that is often very helpful, but first you have to eliminate as much friction as possible.

Even the least businesslike categories are important. Suppose you have this situation:

Trait	You	Your Manager	Match?	Action Needed?
Sense of Humor	Standard (I'm Italian)	He tells Italian jokes. (He's not Italian.)	No	-

Here's a source of potential conflict that could easily ruin a relationship and, as a result, your career. Your manager may not even be prejudiced, but if you are going to be irritated by his jokes, the result will be the same. Hostility cannot be successfully masked for any length of time. There is also no tactful way of telling the person who signs your merit review that you don't like his sense of humor. However, taking the problem into consideration in your planning will go a long way toward preventing a blowup.

After you've completed your analysis of both environmental and personal factors, let a few days pass before you begin to plan formal actions. This gives you some time to think about the implications of what you have learned and to come up with additional items that should be considered.

You won't lose anything by waiting. Even without meaning to change your behavior, this added knowledge will help you to get along better with your manager on a day-to-day basis. For instance, you will find yourself listening more completely to what he or she is actually saying—and not just to what you assume is being said. Most managers will *tell* you precisely what they want if you listen closely enough.

2

You and
Your Boss

PART II:
Make It Work
for You

Having let the information jell, at the end of several days you should have a reasonably complete picture of your boss and yourself. Think carefully about the points of contact and conflict and the reporting relationship. Ask yourself the following questions:

- *Can* I make this relationship work well? A reporting relationship that works well helps both parties to succeed.

- Do I *want* to make this relationship work? There is no point in expending a lot of energy to develop a good reporting relationship if you don't want to be where you are. Use your energy to change positions. (Of course, *wanting* is a relative term. In some cases, managers only *want* to support themselves and their families. If that is your situation, then ask yourself whether your present position is a suitable one for someone with your priorities. It may not be.)

- What will happen if I don't make any adjustments? Will I lose my job—or just my shot at a promotion? Will anything happen at all? (Not all situations are as serious as Alan's.)

Don't Charge—Walk

If you decide to go ahead and invest some time and effort in developing a better association with your manager, *don't* rush into his or her office to share your newly gained insights. Even the most secure manager will be annoyed—or worse, threatened—by a subordinate who marches in one day and announces that he or she is going to fix up their relationship.

Some differences in approach are relatively easy to handle. For instance, if your boss prefers conservative business dress, buy John Molloy's *Dress for Success* or *The Woman's Dress for Success Book* and follow the rules he gives. After work you can change your clothes and wear purple harem pants if you want. Pin-striped suits don't permanently change you; express your individuality on the weekend.

Other differences are more difficult. As each situation is unique, there are no "right" answers. There are, nevertheless, some guidelines that you can apply to your situation.

1. LISTEN

Begin by really listening to your manager in the light of your new knowledge. To the best of your ability try to deliver what your manager asks for. Don't assume that what has worked in the past is what will work now. When in doubt ask questions.

The key as always is to ask the *right* questions. Don't ask general questions such as "What should I do?" That will only convince your boss that you aren't competent. Ask specific questions. For example, if you're being asked to prepare a report, consider the following: "Would you like the detailed analysis or a one-page summary with recommendations?" At the least you will get some idea what your boss wants. Better still, you may spark a discussion that will answer all your questions in an informal way without having to ask them.

Another method is to use examples: "Do you like the type of reporting used in the business service quality report?" This may also lead to a full discussion of what your boss wants. Even if it doesn't, you will be ahead of where you were before you asked.

Be sure you are clear on the process your manager wants. Some managers don't want to know anything about a project between the time it's assigned and the time it's due (note: *due*, not completed). Others want daily progress reports or weekly updates. Make sure you know what type of manager yours is. The manager who expects daily reports of progress will not be happy with you until you deliver them.

If you don't, you will be piling up negatives in your boss's mind that may not be entirely wiped out when you present the completed project—no matter how well it was done.

On the other hand, if your manager doesn't want to hear anything about the project until it is done, and you bring in daily reports, you are only going to be irritating. You will be wasting the most valuable commodity you and your boss have: time.

The solution again lies in adroit questions. Once more using the example of a report ask a question such as: "Do you want to see the first draft or just the edited second version after typing?"

This also gives your manager a chance to decide how often he or she wants to be bothered—something your manager may not have thought about. In which case you look that much better.

There is one caveat. If you run into problems, you may want to make an interim report even to a manager who doesn't usually want one. It is far better to "bother" your manager early than to wait until something is due and then fail to deliver. More than a working relationship can be terminated in that kind of situation. Remember, your manager's boss may be waiting for that report or project—and so on up the line. Your failure could have serious repercussions not just for you but for several layers of management above you. It is only prudent to make sure everyone has some time to prepare and, perhaps, change schedules so that problems can be handled *before* it is too late.

2. COMPROMISE

In addition to asking questions, try to adjust easy-to-correct personal mannerisms and reduce potentially threatening behavior. Don't try to become someone else, however; it won't work. Compromise. Lean toward your manager's convenience but don't forget your own life. If your manager likes early-morning meetings, get up even earlier, come well prepared, do your job well, then reward yourself with a bit of extra time at lunch. That way you won't feel as pressured. You're still conforming to someone else's schedule, but you're easing your own along the way.

If on the other hand you expect to get home a little later than usual because your manager's meetings always run overtime, invite your spouse to dinner at a fancy restaurant near work (or catch a hamburger and a movie). The point is that you and your family will be happier if you accept and plan for (and around) the inevitable instead of constantly having to cancel or change your plans.

3. RECOGNIZE THE UNCHANGEABLE

Here's an example. If your boss is an older man with an old-fashioned European background and you're a young black female dedicated to woman's rights, his courtliness and courtesy may drive you crazy. You have two choices: change jobs or live with his style. Should you choose to live with it, acknowledge that neither he nor you is likely to change. What is good manners to him—such as not wanting you to go alone on a business trip—will make you feel like climbing the walls.

You must restrain the urge toward homicide (murdering your boss is regarded by most experts as a poor long-term career move). You will need to learn how to release your tension and anger. To that end there are two methods of stress control—a general program and an immediate method.

The general method is simple. Most stress-control programs emphasize good health as a basis, with sound nutrition, physical exercise, sufficient sleep and outside interests also important. In addition, plan around your stress times: after a long, stressful afternoon meeting, you might plan that evening to see a new film that's supposed to be funny. If you know a stressful situation is coming up, use the same concept. The night before, do things to take your mind off the upcoming problem. This will not only help you sleep but assure that you are mentally alert to face the stress.

Chart 2.1 gives examples of immediate methods. You will know when you need to use them.

CHART 2.1

SOME IMMEDIATE METHODS OF STRESS CONTROL

You can use most of these methods at your desk. Consult your doctor, stress-control center, or physical fitness center for more information.

- Muscle relaxation (alternate tensing and relaxing)
- Yogic breathing
- Laughter
- Venting—Getting it out of your system. (Tell someone else your problem without expecting the other person to do anything about it.)
- Meditation (borrow an office if you don't have one)
- Physical exercise (go jogging or do aerobic dancing at lunch)

Don't rush into things; allow some time for your changes in behavior to take effect. It is unlikely that you will see an immediate impact, if for no other reason than it will take time for your manager to notice that something has changed. The delay will give you time to become more comfortable in your new role. Time will also allow you to judge what effects your efforts are having on your manager. When you feel confident that you have done all you can and that you are on at least reasonable terms with your manager, you are ready for the next step—*if* it is necessary.

Grabbing the Bull by the Horns: Suggesting Changes in Your Working Relationship

The meeting in which you suggest changes is one of the most difficult steps in the process of putting together a working relationship. It is also the one step that is often unnecessary. If your relationship is working nicely, you don't need it. However, if the relationship between you and your manager is still not working after you have tried to improve it, a direct face-to-face discussion becomes very important. There is no substitute for this step short of finding a new job or resigning yourself to the idea that you will never get along with your boss.

Your approach to the meeting and attitude during the meeting must be carefully planned. The reason you are asking for the meeting is because your relationship is not working; that makes a frank discussion more difficult. And a frank discussion is what you want; you don't want this to become a confrontation. Therefore, you must prepare carefully.

First, suggest the meeting to your manager. Don't make a big deal of it—remember, you want to avoid confrontation. If you make a major issue of the meeting before you begin you will most likely find yourself facing a hostile supervisor. At best, your manager will be unlikely to come with an open mind.

Add the meeting to another meeting. If you can, have the first meeting be something that will act as a lead-in, for example, a status review. Be sure that you will have plenty of time and privacy. Some people find that a lunch meeting is a good format, but be careful. Trying to have a frank and possibly emotional discussion in a noisy restaurant, interrupted by waiters and busboys, can be difficult. (If you feel you must have the meeting over a meal, you may suggest a breakfast meeting. Start early and make sure that you *and* your boss are not expected in at the dot of nine. Any kind of limit negates the big advantage of the breakfast meeting—the business day has not yet begun and neither of you is as likely to be distracted by what's waiting to get done on your desk as you would be at lunch.)

Take written notes to the meeting and use them. No matter how good your memory, no matter how well you think you handle yourself in a difficult situation, bring notes. This meeting may be stressful so let your notes help you. If things are going well and you never use them, fine. But it is far better to have spent the time preparing them and not use them than to take a chance that, under stress, you forget half of what you wanted to talk about. Notes will also help you to keep cool by giving you something to refer to, a structure to fall back on. You are less likely to improvise—and in a stressful situation, improvisation is not the best idea. You are not as likely to present your ideas cogently and—very important—unthreateningly if you have to concentrate as much on what you are saying as you do on how you are saying it. In this step, the *way* you present yourself and your problems is crucial to avoiding confrontation.

Plan just a few items or one major item to be covered. Be specific. "We don't seem to get along" is too general and is unlikely to lead to a productive discussion. Try something such as this: "I don't seem to be clear on the format you want in the Monthly Status Report. Could you point out what I'm doing wrong?" Or: "I understand you're unhappy with the progress of the microfile project, but I'm at a loss what to do differently. I'd appreciate it if you could give me some idea of what you'd like changed."

The point is to start a discussion. By raising a specific point you can start your manager talking, and then you can lead the conversation to more general topics. Most importantly, you are avoiding the head-on confrontation that would destroy the very purpose of the meeting.

When you have said what you wanted to say, stop. Often a meeting such as this will go so well that you will be tempted to bring up additional topics. Don't. This is not a situation where it is advisable to push your luck. If there are additional items you decide you want to cover, wait a bit and then ask for another meeting. If the first one has gone so well that you are tempted to add topics, the second meeting will be that much easier.

If you must talk about specific things your manager has said or done, try to label the items you want to discuss as working methods. This is much less threatening than a critique of management style or personal traits. Nonetheless, always take your manager's style into account. Some managers prefer a soft approach, while others will tell you to cut the bull and get to the point (and some of them will even mean it). There will be enough potential conflict in this meeting; if you adapt your style of presentation to your manager's preferences you will at least defuse some of it. You want to keep the meeting as stress-free as you can.

Finally, be sure to listen very carefully. When your manager asks questions make sure to think your answers through. Choose your words, avoiding ambiguity if you can. You're at this meeting to get solid answers to your questions; answering your manager's questions incompletely or evasively will destroy the climate you are trying to foster. Above all, if you don't know something, say so. This is not the time to wing it. You aren't trying to impress; you are trying to build a sense of trust.

Below is a sample script from a working-together meeting. Susan, the subordinate, has selected one major goal for this meeting: she wants Muriel, her manager, to use the chain of command when assigning work to the staff. At present, Muriel is assigning jobs directly to Susan's people without telling Susan and criticizing their performance when Susan is not present.

MURIEL: That's everything on my list. Your nickel.

SUSAN: John starts his vacation today; he's leaving Roy in charge. He'll be gone for two weeks. The monthly report is almost finished. I'll have a draft of it for you to review tomorrow afternoon.

I'd like to take a few minutes to discuss something you could do to help me. It would be very helpful to me if you would speak with me rather than my managers when you are assigning work.

MURIEL: What do you mean? Are you saying you don't want me to talk to the people who report to you?

SUSAN: No. My staff learns a lot from working with you. I certainly wouldn't want to stop that process. Let me give you an example of what I mean. Last week, you gave Beth several customer problems to investigate with a rush deadline. As you know, she did a good job on the investigations, but she didn't do the weekly statistics which left us all scrambling. I think . . .

MURIEL: This is ridiculous! It's silly for me to waste time when you're in a meeting or traveling and your staff is right here. Those people work for me too!

SUSAN: We all do, of course. I can understand that I am sometimes difficult to find. Perhaps I should call your office more frequently? (Watching carefully, Susan notices that Muriel nods slightly.) I'll try calling every other day around 4:30.

My problem is that when you assign jobs to my people I have no idea what they are working on. In Beth's case, I assumed she was doing the weekly statistics. I can't supervise my department properly and do a good job for you if I don't know what my people are doing. If you would tell me what you want instead of going directly to my staff, I could work the new assignments into the overall work effort.

MURIEL: Well, I can see that it's easier when you know what's going on. I'll try—but when you're away. . . .

SUSAN (compromising logically): I understand that you'll speak directly to the person I leave in charge. That person will be responsible for bringing me up to date.

Reinforcing Your Manager's Behavior

Your manager (most managers, at least) is a human being. Just as you reward your staff to reinforce good work, recognize your manager when he or she demonstrates new behavior at your request. In fact, recognition of your manager's efforts—especially when it has nothing to do with you—can help to build a better camaraderie.

Frequently the higher an executive gets in an organization, the less recognition he or she receives. As salary and title increase, responsibilities and the level of performance demanded also increase. Unfortunately, something has to give, and often it is remembering to give praise. A kind word, even from a subordinate, can have a remarkable effect. As long as you avoid blatant flattery—which tends to be counterproductive—complimenting your boss is an activity where the risk is low compared with the possible reward.

This is not meant to imply that compliments are the road to executive success. There are instances where a superior wants "yes-men," but that is an unhealthy situation and a search for a new position might be in order. This chapter is, though, about establishing and improving a working relationship; appreciation of a job well done is part of creating and maintaining such a relationship.

Choose a subject that has meaning. You might comment when your boss has completed a special project or beaten an impossible deadline. Avoid looking for excuses to give out praise; it will be appreciated more—and mean more—if it is truly deserved.

The Chinese Lunch and the Saturday Sail

Most bosses have a favorite cuisine. Why not order it in for your next working lunch? You are, as always, trying to foster a pleasant working environment and a good relationship. If your boss loves Chinese food and you have Chinese food brought in for that working lunch, it won't cause you to be promoted on the spot, but it is likely that your boss will enjoy the lunch—and you will have applied a little grease to the wheels of the relationship.

Activities outside work can be important too. They offer an opportunity to meet in a less-formal atmosphere. Often the opportunity arises through an invitation to join your manager in some special form of recreation. The Saturday afternoon spent sailing with the boss will reap manifold rewards in friendship and greater on-the-job harmony.

Perhaps most important, shared activities away from the office are a chance to meet and talk without the interruptions and the formalities of the workday. Sometimes there may be an ulterior motive involved and the employee who passes up the invitation may be passing up a vital chance to secure greater cooperation.

Consider the following two cases:

Michael had a terrible relationship with his superior, David. The two of them had totally different management styles, their approach to problems was different, even their outlook on life was different. The relationship was often acrimonious. The only reason Michael wasn't fired was that he ran a technical department very well, consistently turning out superior results. David looked good as a consequence of Michael's work, which predisposed him to put up with the conflicts. (David was also a weak manager; it is likely that a strong one would have reined in Michael long before.)

Nonetheless more time than Michael wished was spent in conflict with his boss. In addition David made no effort to secure the salary increases and title that Michael's work merited.

One thing that especially irked Michael was that David was always asking him to play golf. Michael also played golf, but disliked David so much that he refused to play with him, fobbing his boss off with excuse after excuse. Michael couldn't understand why David kept asking him.

There are several possible reasons why David kept asking Michael to play golf with him. It could have been that David, though a weak manager, recognized there was a problem and was seeking an informal situation in which to talk it over. A round of golf allows time for conversation and for companionship. It is unlikely that David and Michael would become friends by playing golf, but it might help to defuse some of the hostility. Also, the informal, unstressed atmosphere on the course and in the clubhouse could foster the same kind of interchange that takes place at a good working-together meeting.

Even if that had not been David's purpose, Michael was still foolish to refuse. *Michael* could have used the outing to lessen the conflict and work on creating a better relationship. By refusing, he was throwing away an excellent opportunity.

The second case is similar but the manager's purpose was different.

Armand got along quite well with his boss, Joan, but was surprised nonetheless when she invited him to go sailing with her and her husband. Armand had other plans for the weekend, but decided that the chance to spend some relaxed time with his boss was too good to pass up. He went and spent a pleasant day with Joan and her husband on their sailboat.

Some weeks later, Armand was called into Joan's office and offered a promotion. Before inviting Armand out on the sailboat, Joan had decided that Armand was probably the best candidate for the promotion, but she was not completely sure. The day on the boat gave her a chance to observe Armand in a different environment than the formal, structured one of the office. Armand might have gotten the promotion even if he turned down the invitation, but by going, he gave Joan a chance to confirm her choice in her mind.

This does not mean that you should act in a calculated, hypersensitive way if your boss invites you to play tennis, nor conduct an investigation into what your boss likes for lunch. It does mean, however, that you should watch for and consider seriously opportunities to increase the rapport between you and your manager outside of work and to make the work environment more conducive to a good relationship.

Have You Sold Yourself Out?

It may seem that these chapters have been devoted to telling you how to become less of an individual. Not at all. Don't lie, give in, sell yourself short, or become a "yes-man." As a manager, you are being paid to think. If you disagree, say so—but manage the relationship. The only chance you have to be effective and to implement your own ideas is if you are a trusted employee. Since management is a team effort and you have to be a team player, you and your manager need not and should not have an adversary relationship. You are no less an individual if you work to bring about a good work environment, and you are likely to be a happier and more productive one.

It is quite possible for you and your manager to be very different— in style, in approach, etc.—and still be able to work together effectively. Know your manager's likes and dislikes and work with them. One manager will want you to say your piece flat out, without embellishments; another will want 30 pages of analysis and detail; a third will nod now and expect you back in three days with a succinct verbal presentation. It is quite likely that your own style will not match that of your boss. It is not necessary for you to change your style in dealing with your own subordinates, but you should do your best to adapt your presentations to your manager's preferences. You are more likely to get approval of your projects if you present them in the manner your manager prefers.

Often these very differences can work to the advantage of both you and your manager. Some of the finest collaborations, whether in business or the arts, come about because the individuals involved complement each other: the writer helping the speaker, the detail-thinker supporting the big-picture person, the late-night person spelling the early riser. If you are strong where your manager is weak and vice versa, the resulting team can be far more effective than either of you could be alone.

The key is to work together—and people can't work together without compromise. A good working relationship with your superiors is the foundation of being a successful middle manager. Without that relationship, you will expend needless time and effort that could more productively be used in doing your job.

A good working relationship is also a vital prerequisite for successfully managing up.

3

Support Your Boss—
You'll Both Win

Staff support consists of two areas: those things directly related to your job that enable you to function (hiring and employee supervision, budgets, purchasing supplies and equipment, etc.), and those things not directly related to your function that you do to help your boss or the management team. Supporting your boss may include preparing reports for his or her signature, conducting meetings, handling your boss's mail or phone in his or her absence, or anything else you are called upon to do.

Before going any farther, take a minute to think about how you would like to be supported by those who work for you. Now turn that information around and apply it to your boss. What can or should you do?

You cannot expect your manager to support you if you do not give him or her your support. *You* have to supply your boss with the information and tools that make the difference between success and failure, whether they are used in meeting the area's objectives or in presentations to other managers.

There is a side benefit to providing good staff support. Part of the purpose in managing up is to increase your freedom and personal control. The manager who supports the boss—the manager whom the boss can rely on and trust—is the one who will be given the most freedom and the least supervision. The object of this chapter is to ensure that you are that manager.

STAFF SUPPORT—PART ONE
DIRECTLY RELATED TO YOUR FUNCTION

First Things First

The first part of providing staff support is to do your own job well.

Perhaps this sounds obvious, but it's easy to forget, especially for the new manager faced with managing a staff for the first time. The demands on your time can increase dramatically—and there is always the temptation (occasionally the compulsion) to do other people's jobs for them. Your own job can get lost in the shuffle.

You should know the specifics of your position thoroughly. It shouldn't be necessary for your manager to do more than review your completed plans, making strategic changes when necessary. Some managers will insist on doing more, but you shouldn't plan on it. Just as you are being paid to supervise and manage your employees, so your boss is responsible for supervising and managing you. Neither of you is expected to do your subordinates' jobs nor is it desirable that you do so. Conversely you don't want your boss "interfering" with the way you do your job. The best way to avoid that is to do it so well that there is nothing for your boss to interfere with.

The Essentials

To get a handle on your own area, you must have the essentials. Simply stated, there are three essentials: people, money, and objectives.

People are the first essential because you will stand or fall on the basis of your staff's performance. Hire the best people you can. Once you've hired them, pay them fairly. Economizing on salaries is always a false economy; if you have hired the best people, the only way you can hold on to them is to pay them. You must also recognize their accomplishments; while salary is a potent motivator, praise and recognition can make the difference between a satisfied employee and an unhappy one. Prepare your people for promotion—into your job or other appropriate positions. (An irreplaceable manager is just that— not promotable because no one else can do his or her job.) You can support your manager by getting things done through others, but, by definition, you must have help.

Money is the second essential. Prepare your budget and forecasts fairly, accurately, and thoroughly. Ask for what you need and don't try to make unrealistic cost savings. (If you don't get it, at least you have asked. If you don't ask and later find you can't meet objectives for lack of money, you are the only one to blame.) Be prepared to present your area's financial status at all times. Come in within budget. Don't take the attitude that going over budget is expected; at some companies, coming in at or under budget is the major measure of a manager's success. If for some reason you can't stay within your budget, the next best thing is to notify your manager as early as possible—with complete supporting data. You will only make matters worse if you try to hide the ugly truth until the end of the fiscal year.

Objectives are the third essential. Know the corporate objectives and include them in your own. As a manager, you must resist the tendency to consider your area or department as an independent entity. Even if you have no bottom-line (profit) responsibility, even if policy manuals do not mention it, you are expected to do your best to help carry out corporate objectives. Recognizing this and making it a part of your plans will serve you well.

Be sure that the objectives you write do the following:

- Support your manager
- Show your strengths
- Fall within your capabilities

Reporting

Once you have your own area in line, you are ready to support your manager—and make your own life easier—by helping him or her to clearly understand that your area is under control. You do this through reporting.

Few managers can advance without good reporting skills. Through regular, comprehensive reporting, you can give your manager a sense of security and confidence. Without it, you will find yourself constantly bothered by your manager seeking information—information he or she should not have to request.

In the early stages of your relationship with your manager, you will need to report more than will be necessary later on. The start of a relationship is always a learning experience. After you and your manager are comfortable with each other, you will develop a sense of what must be reported and what can wait. There is no hard and fast rule for this. As your relationship grows and you discover more about each other's style of management, the frequency required and the amount of detail you need to include in each report will become obvious. Once again listening to what your manager is actually saying is important. Only by listening will you learn what he or she wants to hear and what can be skipped.

Reports given in writing should as always carefully conform to the format and guidelines favored by your company, division, area, and, especially, your manager. Be aware of any differences that may exist between informal communications—such as reports that only your manager will read—and formal reports that may be passed up the management hierarchy. In some instances, both types of reports will

CHART 3.1

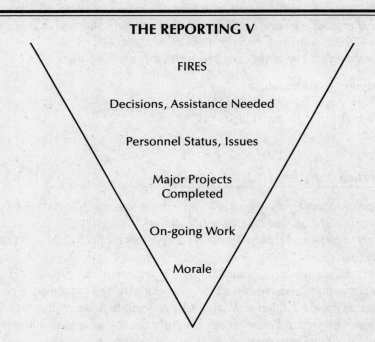

THE REPORTING V

FIRES

Decisions, Assistance Needed

Personnel Status, Issues

Major Projects
Completed

On-going Work

Morale

Report on topics in descending order of importance. Fires are, of course, emergency or unexpected management crises. The two topics at the bottom of the V need not be included during every reporting session, but must be touched on at least every ten days.

be the same; in others, the formal report will conform to a rigid format or require more documentation. Informal reports are often expected to be supplemented by verbal reports or are summaries of meetings or conversations. By their very nature, they will not be as complete as a formal report. If you suspect that a report might be passed on, it is better to do the extra work than to take a chance that an informal—and incomplete—report will represent you to higher management.

Verbal reporting, unless set in format by the type of meeting you are attending or structured by an agenda, should follow a V format, with the most time being devoted to those subjects that are most important.

Selling? I'm a Manager, Not a Sales Rep!

Sometimes it is necessary to sell a report or request. You are selling—or should be—whenever you ask your manager to approve such things as a budget or salary increase. In many cases, your request will be presented in both verbal and written form, often simultaneously. You must be sure to dot all your i's and cross all your t's before entering into these situations. The difference between this kind of reporting and other kinds is that, when you are presenting a budget or a personnel action, you are *selling* your ideas and decisions. It is not uncommon for a manager who does a good selling job when pitching a new project or product to do a bad job on budget and personnel presentations. Usually this is because the project presentation *is* recognized as a sales situation while the others, incorrectly, are not. Chart 3.2 lists some steps you may want to follow.

As with any good sales presentation, some good news up front always helps. Present a successful project or report before you begin a difficult sell. Whenever possible, create a direct need for the person or budget you are proposing. Relate it specifically to your manager's needs or objectives. Too often, a budget or hiring proposal is justified with "I need five new staff members and a million dollars in order to do my job." While this may be true, it is unlikely to overcome resistance. A statement such as "The recent assignment of the cockroach extermination project to our area has caused a reshuffling of work assignments within the department. As a result, we are having difficulty meeting the department objectives in both the artificial cow and the iron duck projects. The additional staff I am requesting will allow continued

CHART 3.2

SELLING YOUR RECOMMENDATIONS

STEP	EXAMPLE
1. Research	• Review previous successful budgets. • Get budget format, if any, from finance department. • Obtain senior management goals to be incorporated in your package.
2. Planning	• Think through the process. • Develop your department objectives and relate them to senior management goals. • Include an effectiveness measurement (unit cost, etc.). • As you plan, *write down* the benefits management will receive if your budget is approved intact. • Have "in your pocket" *but not as part of your proposal* several lower-cost budgets—cutting what you want, not what management wants.
3. Preparation	• Proof-read everything twice. Make more than enough copies. • Make charts or other materials that clearly show the benefits. • Schedule your presentation for the best time of day for your boss.
4. Make your Presentation	• Start with an overview and the benefits, then review details. • Be as calm and quietly enthusiastic as you can be. • If you don't know the answer to a question, say so and get the answer within 24 hours.
5. Follow-up	• Be sure to report results against your new budget. • If appropriate, thank your manager for the support shown.

concentration on the new assignment without falling behind in areas we were able to handle before." The second justification relates the request to specific tasks. This allows your manager to evaluate the additional costs of your proposal against the possible nonperformance or completion of assignments for which he or she bears ultimate responsibility.

Policies and Procedures

Failing to follow procedures is one of the easiest ways to get tripped up in a new position. You and your manager will get almost instant flack from support departments if you deviate from proper formats. There is only one way to avoid this pitfall: you must have a thorough working knowledge of the company policies and procedures. If you are not familiar with these ground rules, become so immediately. Without willing help from support departments, you will find your job becoming impossible; with their help things will be much smoother. It only makes sense to find out the rules before you make mistakes.

Do get copies of all policy and procedure manuals; they can map the ways through and around the system. Even if the manuals are "only for our department's use" or "really quite out of date," try to get copies. Since organizational styles don't change rapidly, they will probably tell you a lot about the organization and the general way things are done—even if they're no longer done precisely that way.

Be careful, however, that you don't assume—even subconsciously— that you can learn everything you need to know from these procedures books. There are two reasons for this. First, policy manuals are frequently out of date or very incomplete; sometimes the old policies may have been changed, or perhaps new situations have called for new policies. These changes and additions ideally *should* be in the manual, but all too often they aren't—and if you follow the manual you will be wrong.

Second, policy manuals, even if up to date, give you only the basics; they don't tell you the customs particular to your division or area. In any society, the way things are done is often as important as what is done—otherwise no politician would ever get reelected.

In many cases you can get the manuals and information you need without taking up your manager's time. Most support departments will be more than happy to spend time acquainting you with the proper forms and methods to use to prepare your budgets, hire and promote

CHART 3.3

WHAT PROCEDURE MANUALS WON'T TELL YOU

The following is a sample of a page from a corporate procedures manual:

CREATIVE SERVICES, INC. POLICIES & PROCEDURES		6.3 Page 6 Rev.7/27/81
CHAPTER 6: Personnel Policies	Supersedes 6.3 Page 6 rev. 1/15/78	
SECTION 3: Managerial Promotions		CONFIDENTIAL

Prepare the form shown below two months in advance of the desired promotion. All sections must be completed and the form approved by the three supervising managers in the direct line of reporting.

⊕ CREATIVE SERVICES, INC. ⊕

PERSONNEL CHANGE REQUEST   VER 9/81-1021

SECTION A

Employee Name_____ I.D.# _____

Current Status:

Title _____ Grade _____ Salary $_____

Date of last change _____ of last salary increase _____

percent of increase _____%

amount of increase $_____

Proposed change:

Title _____ Grade _____ Salary $_____

Date change would take effect _____

SECTION B

Describe the manager's performance during the period covered--especially accomplishments and areas for improvement:

What this page doesn't tell you is that the informal requirements for Section B for any managerial promotions at Creative Services are accomplishments in three areas: financial results, performance against MBO's (management objectives), and at least one productivity improvement. Promotional paperwork submitted according to the sparse directions in the policy manual without the three accomplishments are always returned for "rethinking"— if not rejected outright—even if the candidate is fully deserving of promotion.

your staff, purchase materials, etc. Support departments spend a surprising amount of time dealing with incomplete and improperly filled-out paperwork. When you follow their procedures, you make their lives a lot easier.

For instance, if you take the time to ask, the personnel department will usually explain how promotion paperwork should be completed—because it is easier for *them* if your work conforms to policy. Most likely they will be able to show you samples of requests that were successful. Remember, they generally have no interest in whether a particular person is promoted or not. They *will* be rated by their superiors, however, on the basis of the paperwork in their files and their adherence to promotion policies and salary guidelines. If your requests are in order, they will have no reason to protest and every reason to be cooperative. The same is true of other support departments, from accounting to purchasing. And if you build up a reputation as someone whose paperwork is always in order, you are likely to get more expeditious treatment than other managers who don't bother to follow procedures.

If you can't get help from a support department, ask a peer or someone who works for you to show you successful examples. Be careful to use your own judgment. Improve on what you see—you may not be looking at the best examples. To avoid this, try to get several examples when using this method.

If your peers cannot help you, there is one final method of securing examples. Ask your secretary or your boss's secretary for help; secretaries can be powerful allies. They frequently remember where good examples might be filed and, if the items are confidential (such as personnel recommendations), often know how to secure permission to show them to you. (In cases where the information on an example is confidential, you might suggest they show you a photocopy with the names blanked out. After all, it's style, not gossip, you're after.)

It may sound like a lot of work, but it's better to take the time than to have all your promotion recommendations come back disapproved by a Grade Z clerk in personnel, or discover that you can't get the supply room to replenish your paper clips even though you're a vice president.

There are many areas where you should be sure you know and follow both the formal and informal policies and procedures. Some of the most important are:

- Personnel (including hiring, firing, performance appraisal, poor performance documentation, coaching, etc.)
- Purchasing
- The financial cycle (including budgets, forecasts, monthly reporting, variance analysis)
- Staff recognition
- Training
- Corporate identity standards (logos, signs, etc.)
- Reporting (weekly or monthly reports, daily statistics, quality and timeliness standards)

Even within your own area, good paperwork can be vital. If you present your manager with complete, accurate paperwork and well-designed proposals, you are encouraging him or her to approve it as it stands. Sloppy work, however, invites correction, and once a manager starts to make corrections, there is less resistance to reworking or redoing the entire proposal. Get it right the first time and it is more likely to remain unchanged throughout the approval process.

STAFF SUPPORT—PART TWO
NOT DIRECTLY RELATED TO YOUR FUNCTION

Once you have established that you can do your job *and* report it to your manager in a useful way, you can begin to provide staff support in other areas.

Working with or Becoming the Chief of Staff

Your manager may or may not have a chief of staff. If he or she does have one, the position may be formal or informal. If there is no official chief of staff, you should identify who performs these duties informally. Find out who most often represents the boss at meetings or takes charge when he or she is away. See who among several ostensibly equal subordinates is usually put in the line of reporting on new projects; this is the person who functions as a chief of staff.

The informal chief of staff frequently takes the boss's job when it comes time for promotions. The reason is simple—everyone knows this person can do the job. He or she already does it when the boss is away. This is less often the case with formally designated chief of staff positions. Formally designated chiefs of staff frequently get labelled as *staff* and don't get the chance at the boss's job. It's something to remember: always try to have at least some line (direct supervision) responsibilities to avoid the staff-only designation.

If you can't identify an informal chief of staff, good. You now have the chance to perform these functions. You can help yourself and your manager by becoming the chief of staff—informally. Work into the job. When budgets or forecasts are due volunteer to prepare a sample format. Help your manager prepare presentations or speeches; not only will you have the opportunity to learn, but you can step in in an emergency, which will make you more visible—always a help to a career.

Chart 3.4 lists those functions most often performed by chiefs of staff. These functions fall into three catagories:

- Administration
- Standing in for your manager
- Project work

Some of these tasks may appear to be clerical. They become so only if you let them. For instance, don't make the mistake of becoming a message-taker. Don't just take a message; handle it. Draft responses to incoming mail with your manager's prior approval; send them when you are sure of your solution. Complete the task—then you aren't being a clerk.

If your manager does have a chief of staff (or someone with an equivalent title) or an informal chief of staff, be sure to become well-acquainted. You will be expected to work closely with this person in any case; developing a good working relationship is a key to working with your boss.

Once again, it is not necessary or desirable for you to be obsequious. You can simply express your willingness to be supportive to both your boss and the chief of staff, who will in most circumstances be more than happy to have the help.

Staff Meetings

Staff meetings are a necessary evil, which is not the same as saying all staff meetings are necessary. Anyone who has spent any time in a management position knows some (most?) aren't. Some meetings *are*

CHART 3.4

___

CHIEF-OF-STAFF FUNCTIONS

TASK	COMMENTS
ADMINISTRATION:	
1. Develop formats	• Design the budget package starting with the approach. • Prepare forms for all managers to use.
2. Monitor financial status	• Review the weekly financial summaries. • Investigate problems. • Report only trends and solved problems.
3. Monitor progress on projects	• Set up a milestone calandar. • Review all work as completed. • Assist (and badger when necessary) manager's subordinates in completing tasks as they are due.
4. Set up meetings	• Prepare and circulate agenda. • Arrange meeting place and all necessary tools. • Coordinate attendance.
STANDING IN:	
1. Handle manager's phone and mail during absences	• Whenever possible, finish the transaction.
2. Conduct meetings and interviews	• Since you know what's going on, handle everything you can.
PROJECTS:	
1. Prepare presentations or reports	• Would you sign this if *you* were your manager? If not, redo it. Don't waste his or her time.
2. Do research or problem solving	• Of course, you do this to the best of your ability when asked, but don't always wait to be asked. Look around: what needs doing?

needed, but even in necessary ones it is likely that more management time is wasted than in any other activity. Unfortunately, until someone invents a better method, the staff meeting is the only way to promote discussion and receive reports when more than two people are involved.

First, you can begin by helping organize the meetings. Take charge of arranging for the conference room or making sure audiovisual devices are on hand when needed. Then you can assist your manager, making the time spent in meetings more productive, by preparing for them carefully and using them to show yourself in a good light. Never go to a meeting unprepared. Few circumstances are more embarrassing than being asked for the status of a project and having to admit before your boss *and* your peers that you don't know. Make sure you have *something* to say.

You can aid your manager in meetings by supporting him when he can use it. Since sometimes a meeting can get bogged down, and you shouldn't sit and expect your boss—or someone else—to pull it out. Take an active part: suggest ways of meeting goals; make an effort to work out compromises when a deadlock has been reached. Add humor; often a tense and hostile meeting can become a productive and relaxed one by the introduction of a little humor. Don't overdo it, but it is a rare corporate occasion that cannot bear lightening up. By taking an active part, you can help to see that time spent in meetings is not wasted time. Even if no one notices, you will have saved your own time.

Create

Almost anyone can be a manager. Stand out from the crowd: create. Develop a creative suggestion (a new idea, product, service, procedure, technique, project) at least once a month. Nothing may come of them, but at least you will be seen to be trying. And if one of your ideas is used—and it works—it cannot help but advance your career. One creative suggestion a month is only twelve a year. Do a little extra work over a weekend if you have to and come up with several. Save them up and present them one at a time.

If the Team Fails, You Suffer Too!

Besides supporting your manager, you should always support the team working for your manager. Your manager's superiors will be judging you as a part of that team; your support for the other members of the team is actually support for yourself.

Pinch-hit for your peers and they'll do the same for you. The result will be less worry for you and better results from the management team in general. Also, if you're part of a smoothly functioning team, your work is more likely to receive the attention it deserves. If your manager is too busy explaining budget overages—or why the iron duck sank—there will never be time to consider the new process you'd like to try.

Loyalty

What loyalty do you owe your manager? Like most managerial questions, it evokes both a simple and a complex answer. The simple and logical answer is "as much as your manager shows you in return and your common sense tells you is right." The more complex answer depends upon time and place.

A disloyal employee is not going to go very far under most circumstances. Occasionally, although this is rarer than is commonly thought, someone will get ahead in a company through backbiting and treachery. Generally, the people who act in that fashion soon acquire a reputation—and shortly thereafter find that few managers are willing to have them on a team. No matter what the subordinate's talents, few managers are willing to expose themselves to sharp practice. If you do find yourself in a company populated by sharks, the sensible thing to do is to find another job. The life of a corporate carnivore is often short and violent.

However, this is not a recommendation for blind loyalty. Your responsibility to your own career requires that you not go down in flames with a manager who is acting unwisely or unethically. Some situations present career or ethical considerations that require you to distance yourself from your manager. (For a discussion of corporate ethics, see Chapter 15.) Such distancing, however, is not the same as being actively disloyal, an identification that you should be certain to avoid.

The complex answer to the question, then, is "give as much loyalty as the situation calls for." It is, unfortunately, not an easy judgment call. The higher the rate of change within the organization, the more difficult the answer becomes. In some organizations, it can be a question of whom to be loyal to *today*.

One way to solve the dilemma, perhaps, is to look at your own expectations. If you expect your manager to defend you forcefully when you're right and protect you when you've made a mistake, you should do the same. If your manager fails to live up to your expectations, then you should reconsider how much loyalty he or she deserves.

Most good managers inspire loyalty. If you work for a good manager, the question may never come up. You will act loyally simply because you feel there is no other way to act. Many of the techniques for inspiring loyalty are presented in Section II, Managing Down. It is when these techniques are not being used by your manager that the question of loyalty will arise.

Isn't It Enough to Do My Job?

Of course—but staff support *is* part of your job. It's not listed in many job descriptions, but, nevertheless, it's expected of every manager.

The essence of providing staff support is to do it before being asked. This enables you, as a middle manager, to do a better job of supporting your boss, looking good doing it, *and* retaining more personal control. Consider your areas of responsibility carefully and don't neglect those you share with your peers.

Make yourself look good by making your manager look good. Association with a successful manager has helped many careers to move faster.

4

No: Why You Say It, When to Say It, How to Say It

No. Such a short, simple word, so very hard to say. Even more difficult is saying it at just the right time and place so that it becomes effective. Yet it is one of the most important words in a manager's vocabulary.

Many managers hesitate to say no, even when the alternative is to be assigned more work than they can handle or to be saddled with staff they know are wrong for the job. The reasons for not saying no usually include security ("I'll get fired"), the superman concept ("I can do anything"), or career pressures ("If I don't accept this, someone else will—and they'll look good and I won't").

Paradoxically the reasons why you *should* sometimes say no are those very same reasons. If you don't say no and you take on too much, you are setting yourself up to fail.

If you really think you shouldn't take on a project and you take it anyway, there are three possible results. The "best" result is that you do it despite the problems and do it well. Generally (assuming you were right in wanting to refuse it) this will have been done at the expense of other tasks and your area will fail to meet another set of objectives. Or suppose you have pulled off a minor miracle, and you have accomplished a project with inadequate resources without disrupting your other objectives. Do you really think you will be rewarded for this feat? Chances are you won't, because, by accepting the project without protest in the first place, you said you could do it—and now you have. In other words, you have simply accomplished what you said you could. Why *should* you be rewarded?

In addition you have now established that your department is capable of far more work than anyone thought—and you will get that work, never fear. It's too late to explain that this was a special case; you should have brought that up in the beginning.

The second possible result is that you finish the project, but in a hasty, imperfect manner, or way behind schedule. You may get away with this once or twice, but soon your reputation will suffer. Again, since you failed to bring up the difficulties when you accepted the assignment, *anything* less than a competent result is unacceptable.

The third result is the most likely. You won't complete the project at all. *That* is when you risk getting fired (or put in the corporation's equivalent of the penalty box), not when you say no legitimately. It is a sign of competence, *not incompetence*, for a manager to recognize his or her limits and span of control. The managers commonly known as supermen are usually those who know their limits and manipulate the system to work around those limits. One of the ways they do that is to refuse assignments that are beyond their capabilities or those of their staff. Supermen who fail quickly lose their reputations; saying no helps those reputations stay intact.

As for being fired, your relationship with your boss should never be so shaky that turning down an assignment for legitimate reasons results in dismissal. That is what establishing a working relationship (and "managing up" in general) is all about. A relationship where you can't say no is a bad one, and you should either be implementing the suggestions in Chapters 1 and 2 or looking for another job—possibly both. You *must* have mutual trust; if your boss won't accept your reasons for turning down an assignment, you haven't established that trust.

Sometimes, because of pressure from above, you might end up in a penalty box as a result of a refusal. But ask yourself this: which is worse, to have turned down an assignment or to have blown it—and, possibly, through overextension of you and your staff, have blown other concurrent assignments as well?

It is true that someone else may do the assignment and get the glory. It is unfortunate but less damaging to your career than a failure would be. You can't have all the glory in any case. Management is a team effort.

How do you say no? Prepare the same way you would if you were approaching your boss for approval of a project. Gather your facts, have your reasons ready, request a meeting. Don't make a big deal about it, but if at all possible don't do it in a meeting where others are present. Use these steps in your conversation:

1. Acknowledge the task you're trying to refuse by describing it. (This is frequently called feedback.) If possible, affirm that it *is* a valid task.

2. Say no but leave the door open. Make it easy for your boss to change his or her mind.

3. Give some reasons why you can't or shouldn't perform this assignment. Some valid reasons include:
   - lack of knowledge
   - lack of experience
   - inadequate time
   - inadequate resources
   There are many other valid reasons.

CHART 4.1

SAYING NO

STEP	SAMPLE PHRASING
1. Acknowledge the task	I understand that you would like me to fly to Chicago to present the proposal and the budget for the Tracks System next week. I know the meeting is crucial to the System's success.
2. Say no—but leave the door open	With my current schedule, I can't do the job right. I would like to turn down this assignment.
3. Give some reasons	Although I helped develop the proposal, remember I dropped out of the budgeting process. It would take me at least two full days to be able to present—and especially to defend—the numbers. I have the Norstom proposal to complete by Friday night. In addition, the auditors are due in Accounts Payable on Tuesday and I think I should be available during the audit.
4. Offer alternatives	If the presentation can be moved to the following week, we could do it together—on our way to Philadelphia. If not, perhaps Jack could go. He knows the numbers and I could spend tomorrow afternoon helping him with the product specifications.
5. Reaffirm your commitment	I know Tracks will play an important part in meeting our objectives this year and I look forward to working on the roll-out of the system.
ONLY IF NECESSARY	
6. Lose graciously	I understand. I will go to Chicago. The Norstom proposal will be delayed two weeks and Maria will be acting manager during the audit.

4. Offer alternatives. Your alternatives must be real; otherwise you will sound as if you are pushing your work onto someone else. Some alternatives you might consider are:
   - delay the project
   - assign the project to someone who has more knowledge or experience
   - secure additional resources (usually money, staff, or equipment)
   - restructure the project
   - use previously developed materials
   - cancel the project

5. Reaffirm your commitment to your other objectives and the team.

6. If necessary, lose graciously. (After all, your boss *is* your boss.)

Chart 4.1 gives an example of these steps in practice.

If you find yourself saying no often or frequently being countermanded when you do say no, you may be in the wrong job. Consider your situation carefully. Only you can decide.

Don't jump to conclusions, though. Everyone has to say no once in a while. When you feel you should, consider carefully, think it through, then act. Sit down in your boss's office and simply say "I can't do ——. Here's why: ——."

It may be the hardest thing you will ever have to say. Say it anyway.

5

The Back with the Knife in It May Be Your Own; Don't Lose the Corporate Political Game

It is a typical day at National Disintegration Industries. Birds are singing in the handsome atrium of the headquarters building, and the buds are starting to come out with the early spring weather. Within the climate-controlled, wood-paneled halls of NDI, however, nefarious doings are afoot.

On the fifth floor, known throughout NDI as Executive Row, Gezelda Trueheart, a customer service rep (level 2), slinks into the outer office of Lance Ventlow, your boss's boss. She is passing the time with her frequent lunchtime companion, Mildred Mildew, Ventlow's trusted secretary. She casually mentions that the new system—which you have worked on for a year, your major objective—has made things worse. Later, Mildred passes this tidbit on to her boss.

On the fourth floor, you stop by your boss's office. Your boss is out. You leave the Fastmark report with Mary Martinet, her secretary, stressing how important it is that your boss look it over. It needs to be in the hands of the district representatives within two days. Your boss has to approve it or suggest changes by five o'clock so the report can go into distribution on time. After you leave, Martinet sorts the "In" basket for your boss. There are two other urgent reports besides yours. One is put on top with an "urgent" tag on it. A second is placed on the bottom of the "to do" pile where it will be reached sometime in the next few days. Mary uses your report to protect her desk from a leaking coffee cup.

Back on the third floor, you are frustrated. Once again, the Tunneling Department has failed to provide the statistics for the on-time completion of the monthly all-department report due tomorrow—your responsibility despite the fact that Tunneling is a separate organization reporting to your boss but not to you. You have been castigated five months in a row for the lateness of the report and finally decide to bring up Tunneling's delinquency despite the knowledge that Ron Racecard, Tunneling's boss and your peer, is your boss's favorite. Getting past Mildred, you find your boss in. He listens to you gravely, dismisses the problem as a "personality conflict"—implying it is your fault—and declines to intervene. As you leave, he adds "make sure the all-department report is on time this month."

You return to your office and find a message from Hasty Hagarty, a vice president in sales roughly equivalent in rank to your boss's boss but in a completely different reporting line. You call him back. Hasty has heard you are going to be in San Francisco next week. He confides to you that the sales manager of the San Francisco office—Terry Tryhard, your peer—is a man whose boss—your boss's peer and Hasty's immediate subordinate—thinks will go far in the corporation. Hasty is unsure. He wants you to covertly observe Tryhard and, without telling either Tryhard or the intermediate manager, report back to Hasty what you think. He hangs up with a cheery "See you later." You reflect that, although you don't even work in the same reporting line as Hasty, he is a politically powerful individual who has been known to help or hinder careers.

It would be wonderful to be able to say that there is no such thing as corporate politics! No chance. This introduction, although written humorously, is taken from actual situations. Wherever there are people, there is influence, power, and competition. Add to this brew personality clashes, differing leadership styles, conflicting goals, limited budgets, and rapid change. Yes, Alice, there are lots of good managers but there are also lots of bad managers. You can learn to be politically astute. A thorough understanding of office politics won't save you in all situations, but it can make your working life much easier.

Before beginning, however, you *must* understand that working hard and keeping your nose clean do not guarantee success. As is true elsewhere, many things that happen in corporate life are not even remotely fair. Promotions and raises are often based on favoritism and personal style. So learn the rules *and* do your job well. It will help your career; there are very few senior executives who aren't very skilled at politics. If you can interpret your surroundings, at the worst you will recognize an impossible situation and decide to move before you are asked to do so.

The first step is to learn where the real power is. All vice presidents are not equal; some are more equal than others. You should be aware of the power wielders who affect you.

Power Bases

To learn who has the power in your organization, you will need to study actions as well as organization charts. Begin with an extra copy of the official organization chart and a pencil. First note those you instinctively recognize as having power. Then list underneath each of those people the components of their power which you know about. Components of power include:

- Title or position
- Authority and responsibility
- Size of budget
- Size of staff
- Special knowledge or skill
- Strong leadership skills and the ability to convince others
- Strong personality (often combined with a desire for power)
- Location and size of office—type of secretary
- Reporting line (to whom does the person report)

There will be other signs of power—different in each organization. In some companies, those who travel often or who have memberships in clubs or professional groups, or who eat lunch at certain restaurants are known to have power. If you observe those around you, you will begin to see what the signs are.

Influential Power

After you have completed your listing of power bases, look for the points of influence. To whom do those in power listen? Whom can't the meeting be held without? Whom do you wait for and whom do you start without? Who goes to lunch or for a drink together? More than one manager has accomplished more using mutual commuting time than during office hours. Whomever those in power listen to or consult also have power: the power to influence. Draw lines indicating influence on your chart.

Secretaries and administrative assistants often have considerable influential power. Even the most senior executives frequently listen to their secretaries' opinion of other employees and prospective employees. Some secretaries maintain their boss's calendars and screen their calls. It behooves you to treat secretaries with the professional respect and courtesy they deserve. They are often some of the hardest working individuals in the organization. Recognize them and they may be able to help you; at least, it won't be your report that ends up on the bottom of the pile with coffee on it. If you don't know your boss's secretary, make that your first order of business *tomorrow*.

Passive Power

Many people think of power in the active sense: the power to do, to accomplish, to act or to get others to act. Passive power—the power to stop something—is just as real, as you will know if you have ever tried to implement an advertising campaign the legal department didn't approve or to obtain an office computer the purchasing department didn't like. List the "stoppers" on your chart. (Although not true in all cases, think about these areas: legal, audit, purchasing, standards, quality delivery. There may be others.) Get to know them and to understand their policies and procedures. You can't fight city hall but you *can* learn how it works and conform to the system as much as possible. These areas have been given a responsibility and, in most cases, they are doing their jobs. Here, too, common courtesy (which is really rather uncommon) will stand you in good stead. When you must make an exception, it will be a legitimate one. Both you and the group whose approval you need will know it and you can alert them before hand—along with the reasons why the exception is important.

Entrenched Power

Particularly in very large and very small organizations, there is a fourth kind of power that comes from having "been around forever." There is strength in knowing what has been tried before and where the bodies are buried. Longevity may also confer some ability to influence; senior managers will at least listen to old friends. In big organizations, entrenched groups may also be large and full of inertia. It isn't that they can't move quickly, but they rarely do. It is frequently difficult to find any leverage points to use with an entrenched group; they can't be hurt nor are they motivated by outside advancement. Their needs are filled from within. Take whatever help you can get from entrenched groups and realize that you'll have to do yourself whatever else you need. Mark any entrenched power on your chart. (Training, personnel, and systems are good places to look.)

Other Kinds of Power

There are other kinds of power: those with a reputation, such as a fast tracker; those who are on a power trip and manipulate others because they enjoy it; in technical companies the genius inventor who may know nothing about administration but must be catered to; relatives or lovers of important executives; etc. Many of these will not appear at all powerful according to an organization chart but may have considerable clout—especially of the passive kind—or an ability to influence decisions by either supporting you or opposing you. As with other power bases, use discretion and intelligence in dealing with them. Servility should never be necessary (if it is, unless you enjoy it, find yourself another company), but awareness is. If you are aware, you will never be blind-sided. You still may be tackled, but if you see it coming, you can, at least, prepare.

You've Got All This Wonderful Information—What Do You Do with It?

Chart 5.1 is an example of the way your completed power chart might look. Once you have completed it, remember that the seats of power change often and the nuances and relative positions can change on a minute-by-minute basis. Use your chart to help you interpret what is really going on and to recognize who really makes the deci-

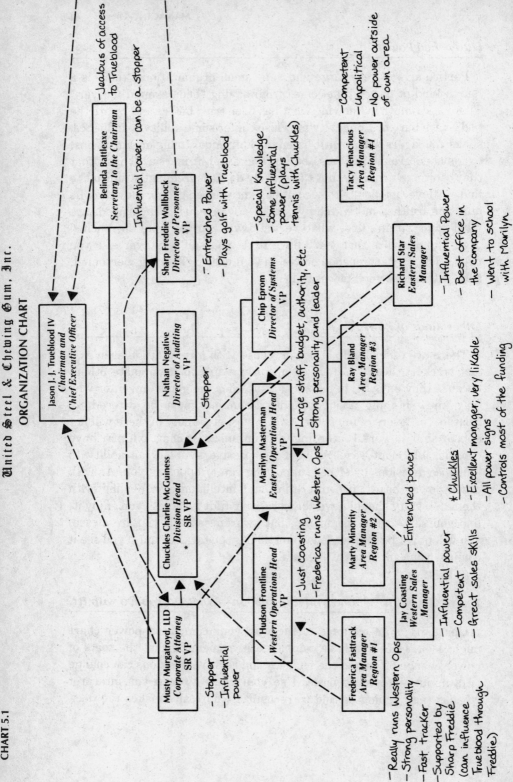

CHART 5.1

United Steel & Chewing Gum, Inc.
ORGANIZATION CHART

sions. Spend your time and make your presentations accordingly. While you will continue to secure approvals from the nominal executives in charge, informally, before you ask for the official sign-off, get the go-ahead from the real decision-makers. Then you can say something like "I ran this by Joe yesterday just to see how it would fit with his plans and he thinks it's a good idea." Since you know the "decision-maker" is going to ask Joe anyway, you've just saved yourself some time. Don't waste your efforts where they won't help you.

Look at your own power. Can you enhance your power base by working towards any of the components of power listed above which you don't already have? Can you increase your influence? This is a slow process, but if you work at it you will make progress. Just as you studied the style your boss uses, look at the style used by those who have political power. If you feel comfortable with that style, good. Emulate it while, of course, remaining an individual. If you really don't like the style of those in power, you may be in the wrong organization. You may want to start looking for another job.

One warning before you continue, do *not* abrogate the chain of command just because someone in that chain doesn't appear to be powerful. That person still has the responsibility for the position he or she holds. In chart 5.1, for example, Frederica Fasttrack should not go directly to Chuckles McGuiness as if Hudson Frontline did not exist unless okayed specifically by Hudson.

Just a few more words on this topic. Protocol is important. Ask someone's manager *before* asking him or her to assume a new task. And be sure never to omit one person in a line of reporting from a carbon-copy list. (Once again, looking at Chart 5.1, you wouldn't copy both Jason Trueblood and Chip Eprom without copying the person in the middle, Chuckles McGuiness.)

Looking Good

Develop a personal style. Although style is not everything, those who look powerful are frequently accorded more respect and help than those who don't. Pay attention to the way you dress, the briefcase you carry, even the pen you use (expensive, of course). Get the best secretary you can. Be sure your telephone is answered cordially and that accurate messages are taken. Your correspondence, both internal and external, should be carefully proofread and accurate gramatically. (Of course, you must also have something worth saying, but here we are talking about style.) If you don't have a secretary, do these tasks yourself. Set standards for the typing pool to use when preparing your materials. Set up your office so that it looks professional and as rich or elegant as you can manage. If you don't have an office yet, do the best you can with your desk or cubicle. Buy small furniture if you must. At all costs avoid cuteness and vulgarity. If you must have cute figurines or calendar pin-ups, put them in a drawer.

What others see (of you) is what you get (in the way of image).

Are You Your Job?

Psychologists have developed a very useful technique for helping executives deal with the strains of corporate political life—distancing. Distancing is just what it sounds like: keeping yourself a little remote from the corporate world. When you are criticized for your work or your actions, remind yourself that it is *your work* or, at most, *your corporate image* that is being criticized. The essential *you* is not being judged. Remember that you can produce an ineffective report without becoming a horrible person, and that people are frequently fired for reasons other than incompetence. (For example, you might be fired because you have a personality conflict with the boss or because the boss wants to replace you with someone else, perhaps an old friend. During mergers, takovers, and relocations, people are often severed because they are no longer needed and not because they are performing poorly.) If you make use of distancing, you must use it all the time, not just when things are not going well. Although it may seem strange, when you are promoted or complimented, you must say to yourself: this is an evaluation of my efforts at work, not of me as a person. Certainly you should be pleased, but leave some distance, which will help you to retain your sanity and health in times of stress.

Are Grapes from the Office Grapevine Sour?

As they spread information, people generate stories, add gossip and speculation, and contribute enriching details. Company employees are no different from other people in this respect. Thus, the very tantalizing rumor mill. Although sometimes wildly wrong, office rumors are often, surprisingly, on the right track. A skilled observer will be able to analyze rumors—based upon his or her knowledge of the power structure and experience with the company—and take actions accordingly. Since forewarned is forearmed, you will want to make use of the grapevine. Listen carefully to what you hear and consider the source. How likely is your informant to have learned something real? What was the original source of the information? What grudges, sour grapes, or gossip may have been added? In the past, how reliable has the information from this person been? Act accordingly.

(If you have a good secretary and have a good working relationship with him or her, you may find he or she is able to provide you with information unattainable elsewhere. Like sergeants in the army, secretaries seem to know everything about what is going on in a corporation—often before their bosses. Think about it—who types all those confidential memos?)

If you want to receive the news, you will also have to share. Reward those who give you the "latest." Be careful, however, about *what* you share with others; don't share truly confidential data. (Unreliable managers are not promoted.) Make it clear when you're gossiping and when you're passing on news. Try as far as possible to pass on information rather than your conclusions. Your conclusions, if they are right, are part of your competitive edge. If they are wrong and you pass them on they may come back to haunt you. Don't become a stress passer just for the sake of sensationalism. If you pass stress you will have your just desserts when your staff becomes too upset to work! The grapevine can help or hurt you; participate wisely and it will become another tool for success.

What Do You Do When Asked to Audit the President?

How do you handle political problems? A political problem is similar to any other kind of problem; you can learn how to solve it. Certain steps can be followed and prerequisites must be established. The prerequisites are a certain amount of intelligence, the ability to analyze and to communicate effectively, and an understanding of the political power in your organization (which you should already have if you keep your political organization chart up to date).

When confronted by a disaster, use these steps:

1. The first thing to do is to keep from going off half-cocked. As

Mohandas Gandhi said "When you are in the right, you can afford to keep your temper. When you are in the wrong, you cannot afford to lose it."

2. Then begin to learn as much as you can about the problem. Speak directly to as many of those involved as possible. Since most political disasters turn out to be tempests in teapots, don't be belligerent before you know the story. Frequently, all it takes to clear up the problem is a good listener.

3. If it does take more than listening, gather enough data to make a decision—but don't wait too long. Time will probably make the situation worse rather than better. Think it over; use your managerial skills. Try to be dispassionate. What would you recommend if you weren't involved?

4. Now consider your own position. Are you right or wrong or (more likely) somewhere in between? How much power do you have? Who else is involved? What can you gain? What will you lose if you do nothing? How recently have you thrown your weight around? (No one likes a bully!)

5. Seek advice if you have a mentor or godfather. (See Chapter 7).

6. Decide what to do. Settle your problems directly with the person causing them. Don't go to someone's boss without at the very least having tried to solve the problem with him or her directly.

7. Before implementing your plan of action, develop a sales strategy. List the benefits of your solution. Save face for as many of those involved as possible—yourself first!

8. Take the action you planned. Stick to your plan unless the situation changes and remember to practice distancing.

Happy Endings?

Meanwhile back at National Disintegration Industries, work and disaster proceed apace. What would you do if you were there? As with any situation in real life, there is more than one answer. Here are some suggestions.

Lance Ventlow mentions to your boss that your new system doesn't seem to be working as well as he had hoped. Nothing specific; just a feeling. Your boss calls you in. You respond calmly, referring to the weekly and monthly status reports. You also suggest that both your boss and Lance join you for a system demonstration early next week. Because you know that Gezelda Trueheart influences Mildred who in turn influences Lance, and because Gezelda, despite her slinking about, does know the system well, you select her to do the demonstration. (You don't know that Gezelda passed the downer to Mildred and Lance—that's too good to be true!) After the demonstration and a review of the statistics, Lance seems somewhat mollified. You make a mental note to be sure to highlight system performance during the next few months.

Your boss's secretary, Mary Martinet, may be a more difficult nut to crack. After you find that your report did not make it to your boss's desk (and this is not the first time this type of thing has happened), you resolve not to leave important papers with a deadline in Mary's control again. You will deliver them yourself or have your secretary keep trying (unobstrusively) until your boss is in. In order to develop some type of working relationship, you remain on the lookout for things that Mary does well and compliment her (only) when appropriate. You also include her in some of the casual conversation that takes place outside of your boss's office—sharing some of your success stories with her.

Ron Racecard is still not providing you with the tunneling statistics on time. After some thought and discussion with your mentor, you decide to set up a process to gather statistics including all areas supposed to be in the report. You will include a timeliness section in the report itself showing when each area reports its data. In this way you are not pointing your finger at Ron—only treating his area just everyone else's. You drop by with each of the managers to discuss the new procedure. During your discussion with Ron you make it very clear that his area will look bad if he continues to be late.

Finally, before you leave for San Francisco where you have been asked to observe Terry Tryhard, you meet Hasty Hagarty in his office. You tell him that you are very uncomfortable with his request but would like to be able to help him out. You add that, since Hasty is in sales and you are in operations, you are not sure your opinion would be valid. Without commenting, Hasty picks up the phone and calls your boss. He requests your help and "opinion in evaluating the sales effort in San Francisco." Hasty puts on the speaker phone so that you can have a three-way conversation. After some discussion, you all agree that you will report only observable facts from the trip. Hasty will draw his own conclusions. A compromise to be sure, but many political solutions are.

National Disintegration Industries will carry on disintegrating, never fear. When you are caught with your back to the wall, the most important thing to do is to think before you act. If you are fully aware of the political environment around you, that thought should be productive.

6

Blow Your Own Horn

This chapter will deal with two specific situations for those who want to stay with their current employer: how to ask for a raise and how to get a promotion or different position. If you have decided you don't want to work for dear old Amalgamated any more, this won't help you. (It will help you once you've found another job though.)

"Uh, Boss, I Deserve (Gulp) a Raise"

How many people ever find the courage to actually ask for a raise? And of those who do, how many do it correctly? Don't knock yourself out trying to guess the answer— very few actually ask for a raise. And of those few, the success rate is still smaller.

Why? Because most people go about it wrong. There are nine steps to successfully asking for a raise. If you follow them your chances of actually getting the raise will be markedly improved. And even if you don't, at least you won't get kicked out of the boss's office for having the temerity to ask.

"She's going in to see Mr. Hughes for a raise."

Step 1

Deserve it. Earn the money you receive now. If you aren't currently doing this, stop reading. Work harder at your job, and, when you are carrying your own weight, come back. Then make yourself even more valuable; begin to be worth more than you're earning. (Don't wait too long to implement the remaining steps.)

Step 2

Carefully monitor your own performance, especially in those areas monitored by your boss and others. Complete your objectives (MBOs) and be sure that you document your achievements carefully; once again presentation counts. Make sure it's letter perfect. Meet your budget and submit your financial-status reports on time with clearly written supporting data. *Exceptions:* If you are not going to meet a goal, think through the circumstances. Present the next best solution (the best solution is to meet the goal) as soon as possible. Bad news is worse when it's too late to do anything about it.

Step 3

Record your achievements periodically—at least once a quarter and preferably once a month. If you have no formal reporting requirement, write a memo to file, copying your manager. It will help to remind your manager of your accomplishments, and it will also help you build a case later on if necessary. (You'll probably use it to prepare budgets and plans for the future too. This is an indispensable tool!) Not too often (about once every six months), write a memo with fairly wide distribution citing a particularly impressive accomplishment. A sneaky way to do this without sounding like you are boasting is to compliment your staff on their—and your—success.

Step 4

Make sure that others recognize your worth. Do what you say you will. Socialize occasionally and talk a little shop—even if you think your co-workers are nerds. Be sure to keep your mentor or godfather up to date. When you've done something extraordinary for someone *and* he or she thanks you, ask him or her to write you or tell your boss. But don't go around asking for compliments. (Asking someone to let your boss know that you accomplished something praiseworthy is not the same thing as fishing for praise in general.)

Step 5

Meet with your boss at least every three months to discuss your performance informally. Don't make a production out of the meeting. If everything is clicking, a simple "I'm feeling good about my performance. I think I'm exceeding my objectives. How do you feel?" will be fine. If you have any doubts, come right to the point. "Would you spend a few minutes giving me your assessment of my performance over the last few months?" Don't ever *assume* you are performing well.

Step 6

Learn everything you can about the salary structure and administration in your company. (Sources include your manager, your peers, and the personnel department. Try to verify information given by your peers—they could be wrong.) Be sure you know what grade or level you are, what the salary range for your level is, what the guidelines for salary increases are, what the guidelines for timing of increases are, and any other information that appears pertinent. Determine what you should receive according to the book. If possible learn what types of exceptions—if any—are made. (In some companies, past experience in the CIA might be a help in uncovering this information; don't despair—persevere.)

Step 7

Learn what other companies pay for positions similar to yours. Read the want ads, talk to your friends, read salary studies in business magazines, ask acquaintances at professional meetings or seminars. Your company may or may not be influenced by your market value, but it is important that you know.

Step 8

Think about steps one through seven from your manager's point of view. Do you deserve a raise? Who else may your manager have to consider from a limited budget? If you deserve a raise and have followed all of these steps, it will probably come without your having to ask for it. If not, you are well prepared to ask for it.

Step 9

Meet with your manager to request the raise. Before the meeting think through all of your options. How strongly do you feel about what you deserve?

But What Do I Actually Say?

An example may help you rehearse your own situation. (Here, as elsewhere, practice does pay off—especially if you are nervous.) Jennifer is just concluding a meeting with her boss, Ahmed, and plans to ask for a salary increase three months before her annual salary review would normally take place. It is now seven and a half months since her last increase and she knows that it takes at least a month and a half to process a raise for a manager. The wage guidelines at Miscellaneous Manufacturers allow for increases after nine months under exceptional circumstances. She has been ready to present her case for the last two weeks and has been waiting to find just the right moment. Ahmed is in a good mood and she knows that his boss, Frank, commented favorably to Ahmed on her sales presentation on Monday.

JENNIFER: I'd like to have a few more minutes of your time if possible.

AHMED: Okay. What's up?

JENNIFER: I'd like you to consider putting me in for a raise in March—even though it would be nine months since my last increase instead of twelve.

AHMED (looking uncomfortable and annoyed): Impossible! It's against the salary guidelines. You know we can't make exceptions.

JENNIFER: I understand your concern that we follow the rules, and it will be your decision, of course, but I feel I have some good reasons for making this request and would appreciate the opportunity to present my case. The Personnel Policy Guide does have a policy allowing nine-month raises under certain conditions.

AHMED: Go ahead, but I only have about ten minutes. The monthly report is due tomorrow.

JENNIFER: It has been four months since I took over the support services department. I now fully understand the area and have proven my ability to manage it. We've met all of the quality and timeliness standards for two months running, *and* the backlog has been reduced to one day. Support services added considerably to my responsibilities without any increase in pay or title.

AHMED: What happened to that person who wanted more responsibility?

JENNIFER: I did and still do want more responsibility. I think my performance continues to show that I am capable of handling it. At the same time, I think I deserve more money in proportion to the increased load I am managing. Last month we reviewed my MBOs and I was on target with all of them except the Smith Sales Campaign—which Frank cancelled. I'm still on target and I'm five percent under budget. You and Frank were pleased enough with the sales program I developed to ask me to present it to the executive committee. (Jennifer notes that Ahmed is a little more relaxed and seems to be agreeing.) Finally, my salary is just barely above the minimum for my grade level and is low for similar jobs in other manufacturing firms. Other managers here. . . .

AHMED: It is none of your business what others here make. Some have been here longer than you. Comparisons of this kind are not productive.

(Jennifer doesn't agree but judges it better not to contest the point now. Better to lose the point and win the raise.)

JENNIFER: I realize that there may be things beyond your control which make my request impossible to grant. All I am asking for is your careful consideration.

AHMED: I'll think about it.

JENNIFER: Thanks. I'd better see what's happening on the line and let you get to the monthly report.

When you actually meet with your manager, don't make it a confrontation. Don't start by threatening to leave the company if you don't get what you want; what will you do if your manager says fine? It would certainly end the discussion, wouldn't it? It's not necessary to start strong; you can always get stronger.

Put together a rational case with very strong supporting evidence; if you've been following the steps above you'll already have it. Acknowledge the rules and ask for what you think is fair. Be aware it's likely that your manager will feel threatened. Be decisive, ask firmly, but give your manager time to think before responding. Avoid putting your manager in a box where he or she has no options. Since it may not be possible for your boss to give you an answer right away, don't force your boss to say no when his or her inclination might be to consider your request. Above all make it clear that it *is* a request—a strong request, yes, but *not* a demand. If you demand, your manager may feel the need to refuse in order to maintain what he or she perceives as the prerogatives of authority. A request is not threatening. If your manager turns you down, then you can look elsewhere. When you get another job offer, you can always reopen negotiations, knowing you have the option of leaving.

My Boss Hides Behind Wage Guidelines; What Do I Do?

First, do (or redo) your homework. Find out everything you can about the guidelines. Do they apply to everyone? How strictly are they enforced? How long will they apply? Then think about nonstandard (not included in the paycheck) ways in which your manager might compensate you. Don't discount this option too quickly. Some of these might be worth much more than you could ever get in salary. Consider compensatory time off (four extra Fridays off can make for four great weekends), advanced-skill courses (which may bring you future earnings), travel to exotic locations for meetings, and anything else you can think of. (If you go this route for any length of time, be sure you can document these benefits on your resume so you are not judged by your low salary.)

Visit your manager again. Restate your case, carefully explaining the other exceptions you found or the reasons why you deserve to become an exception. Listen to his or her response. If the response is still negative, there isn't much you can do as long as you work for that manager and the salary policies stay in effect. You now have a decision to make; you always retain the option of changing jobs.

There are many types of objections similar to the wage-guideline bit that your boss may raise. Do your best to think of potential objections and answers to those objections before your presentation. Chart 6.1 lists some common objections and possible responses.

Sometimes the very act of asking for a raise—however much it may be deserved—puts your manager off. It may even make your relationship worse. This reaction is not rational, but some managers are less secure than others. The decision to ask for a raise should be a political one, and by its very nature should *help* not *hurt* you. Study your manager before you begin. If you decide that making the request will

CHART 6.1

═══

OVERCOMING OBJECTIONS TO YOUR SALARY INCREASE

Before countering any objection, be sure to restate (thereby acknowledging) your manager's concern. Be careful not to overreact.

OBJECTION	POSSIBLE RESPONSES
"We can't make exceptions."	• List some exceptions you are aware of. • Review pay scales in your industry. (Check with your friends, the career center at your local library, and business magazines.) • If company policy provides for some exceptions, discuss them.
"If I do it for you, I must do it for everyone."	• "If I work harder or have more responsibility than others, I should be compensated accordingly."
"There's no money in the budget to cover it."	• "Over the past year, I've saved the company $200,000." • "I know money is tight, but I'm far cheaper than a consultant." • "I plan to be around for a while. I think the return on your investment will more than justify itself." • (If necessary) "I can save the difference in my own budget."
"Your work doesn't warrant an increase."	• First make sure it does. • Review your documentation and raise your daily profile. • "Obviously, I thought it did. Would you spend a few minutes reviewing my performance and explain what more I must do to deserve a raise?"
"The politics just aren't right now."	• This is one of the most difficult to fight. It may be true—and have nothing to do with your performance. If your relationship with your manager is good, enlist his or her help. This is one of the times your godfather (see Chapter 7) can really make a difference.

| "No." | • This can mean one of three things: (1) your performance doesn't warrant it, (2) your boss can't swing it, (3) you have more serious problems than the question of a pay increase. If no raise will be forthcoming, it is very important to determine the reason. It may help you to resolve problems you didn't know you had. If the reason has nothing to do with you, you may wish to ask for other perks (additional training, vacation, or travel, for example) in lieu of money. |

Make the best case you can. Nevertheless, in the final event, it's your manager's decision. You always have the option of seeking employment elsewhere—either inside or outside the company that currently employs you.

damage you, don't do it. Instead continue to perform well and to keep a high profile; decide whether to stay or to look for another, more rewarding position. Perhaps your manager will pleasantly surprise you.

If you make the wrong decision, ask for the increase, and somehow incur the wrath of your manager, carry on as though nothing has happened. Usually if your performance continues to be at or above standard *and* you don't mope, you can bring your boss around. Good luck.

I'd Like to Be the Director of ———— (You Fill in the Blank)

You may want to be the director of marketing; but, if you are now the manager of purchasing, how do you get there? You might be the high mucky-muck of widget public relations, but how do you become the lord high mucky-muck of widget public relations? Or you may wish to move laterally from finance to sales, how do you do it? All of these are changes in position: a lateral change in field; a drop in grade that moves you out of a box and back into a fast-track career path.

The first key to selecting and working towards the right position is to be career minded. A job is something you do between nine and five (no matter how much you're paid) because you need to put bread on the table. A career puts bread on the table too, but it consists of a series of *planned* positions from which you also get some satisfaction and enjoyment. Some positions may be more enjoyable than others, but the key is that you are working according to a plan (which may change from time to time). You may try things you thought you would like and be disappointed, or, quite the reverse, "fall" into the perfect position by accident. Since most careers are built upon a series of positions, the question becomes: how do I get the position I want?

It is important to recognize that career moves need not, in fact, should not always be promotions. Lateral and even temporary "downward" moves may enable you to learn a new skill; work with an excellent mentor; or obtain field, executive-office, or international experience. Look around carefully and try to have several "next steps" in mind. Preparation and flexibility will enable you to move quickly should opportunities arise.

Once you have selected a position towards which you wish to work, you can begin to develop a plan, the first element of which should be a commitment to yourself. You must decide if you and your future are worth the investment of extra work. When you are working towards a new position, you must give more than 100 percent. Indeed you must still give 100 percent to your current job in addition to working towards the new one. No one will take a chance on you or promote you if you are not performing well where you are.

While you are at it, prepare your successor. When you can point to a capable successor, your manager is much more likely to move you. Your successor can also help you with the work load while he or she is learning, thus freeing you to do the extra work required. Basically, that extra work consists of *learning*. You'll need to know as much as you can about the new area so that you can sell yourself in person and on your résumé. Use some of the techniques below to learn as much as you can about the position you aspire to.

● Get to know the people who work in the area you wish to join. Socialize with them if possible. If you can't meet those people in your company (because, for example, they are at a different location), try to meet others in that field from competitive or similar companies. (For instance, if you want to be a customer-service

CHART 6.2

EXAMPLES OF SUCCESSFUL CAREER PATHS

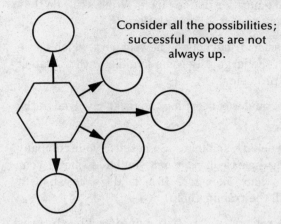

Consider all the possibilities; successful moves are not always up.

1. Lateral

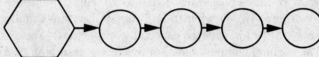

2. Vertical

3. Mixed

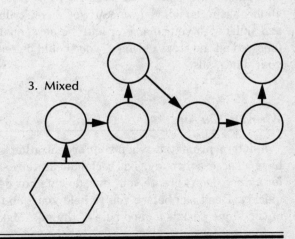

manager for an airline, you can learn a lot from the customer-service manager of a hotel or car-rental company.) Observe those you meet. How do they dress? What do they talk about? What magazines do they read? What type of education do they have? What skills do they have? What can you learn from talking with them?

- Subscribe to the professional journals or newspapers which serve the area. Begin to learn the jargon. Become familiar with the latest trends and the current problems.

- Purchase and read basic guides concerning the tasks involved in the new position.

- Take night courses or weekend seminars. Sometimes your company will pay for this training—particularly when you have shared your career objectives with your manager. If not, do a cost-benefit analysis. How much will the training help?

- Try to get copies of the reports and statistics produced by the area you want to move into. First learn to interpret them, then learn to prepare them. If you wish to be promoted within the area you are currently working, this is especially important. You can make a start at earning the new position by slowly assuming (with permission, of course) some of the duties. (If you are an informal chief of staff, you will be doing this automatically.)

Having done all of this, you are now ready to write your résumé. (Yes, use a résumé even for an internal move; it is a good selling tool.) Emphasize the skills and knowledge you have that will be most applicable in the job you want. If you haven't already, share your plans and skills with your manager and the personnel department; if you've followed all the steps outlined, you should be ready to sell yourself *and* your new skills.

When Do You Ask?

Ask for a promotion when your organization is in good shape and you have a successor ready. The technique is very similar to that of asking for a raise. Don't create your own downfall by demanding too much too quickly. Don't ask before you've held your job for a reasonable length of time (one year is a good rule of thumb). Make sure your résumé is

CHART 6.3

====================

ASKING FOR A PROMOTION

Prepare your case thoroughly beforehand and select the right time to present it.

1. Explain the reason for the meeting and ask for sufficient time to present your case.

2. Review the general healthiness of your area and the preparation of your suggested successor. Go gently here; the choice of a successor may not be your decision.

3. List the reasons you feel you should receive the promotion, including past accomplishments and current skills and knowledge.

4. Thank your manager (if at all true) for the support and training he or she has given you.

5. Rest your case and give your manager time to decide.

6. If the decision is in your favor, begin right away (after you've had your champagne, that is) to build bridges between your current and new positions.

7. Prepare to leave a clean, organized shop for your successor.

====================

ready and reflects the work you have done in the new area. Ask only when you think there is a reasonable chance of success. As usual in a selling situation, choose a time when your boss is not pressured and in a pleasant frame of mind. Present your case as thoroughly as you can and then let your manager make a decision. Chart 6.3 summarizes the steps to follow during your conversation.

What Do You Mean "The New Job Should Be Enough"?

Should you accept a promotion without a raise? It depends on what is in it for you. How much do you want or need the money? How much more of your time and energy will the new position require? Will you lose the opportunity if you insist on a raise? What is the company rule? (Some companies, for example, require that you hold the new position for six months before receiving a salary increase, based upon the theory that it takes at least that long to learn the new job.) When *will* you receive a raise?

So, should you accept a promotion without a raise? In general, the answer is yes; it is a step in the direction you want to go, and money usually follows. But you will have to evaluate each situation individually.

It's Never Wasted Effort

You may find, after doing all or some of this research, that you don't think you want the job after all. Don't despair; it hasn't been wasted effort. You're still ahead: it is far less painful to find out this way than on the job!

If you fail to get the job you want, or don't see a job you want, there is nothing necessarily wrong. A career need not always go up. Lateral moves, for example, can provide a satisfying series of very different type positions. Change prevents staleness; learning a new area can revive a sense of freshness and enjoyment.

Okay, You've Got What You Wanted

Many times in a manager's career he or she will be under intense scrutiny, for example, in the aftermath of a raise or promotion, or even a lateral move to a new position. If you've gotten a raise, remember that a lot of people—senior people—had to approve that raise. Your name will be, at least for a while, very familiar to them. If you have a new position, you will be under close observation not only by senior management but by your new subordinates.

Certainly this is no time to sit back and relax. Celebrate your good fortune with friends or loved ones, but you are going to have to work hard. A tendency to sit back and bask for a bit will quickly lead to sloppy work. Perhaps you don't care how others perceive you now that you've achieved the position you wanted? Remember, you might want another raise or promotion someday.

Do your job well, document what you're doing, and continue to learn enough about your environment to take advantage of sudden opportunities.

The time spent will serve you well.

Never Miss an Opportunity to Promote Yourself

The focus in this chapter has been on what you can do to help yourself from within your company, but you shouldn't forget the outside world. If the opportunity arises and you are good at it, make a speech, teach a class, or write an article. (If you're not good at them, learn the rudiments of these skills, and they will help you in your career.) If no opportunities arise, there are many ways to create them. Several readily available books make excellent suggestions for creating personal promotional opportunities. In any case join the appropriate professional organization for your specialty. If you are a generalist, join the local business lunch club, a university study group, or an equivalent group. Professional stature never hurt anyone. Your boss may be impressed; certainly others in your company will be.

And, should your internal strategies not work, these credentials should help you find another position.

7

Mentors and Godfathers

Most people like to help others. Even the most powerful are generally flattered when asked for their expertise or experience. Mentors and godfathers are senior managers who help you to develop and advance in your career. They must be senior to you in either rank or experience (or both) in order to be of help.

A manager may have several different mentors or godfathers during the course of a career, even if the manager spends his or her entire working life within the same company. It's also quite possible to have both a mentor and a godfather at the same time.

Despite some similarities the mentor and the godfather are two quite different entities. The mental images conjured up by the two terms might seem exotic but contain an element of truth. Mentors are seldom white-robed guru types, but they do perform some of the same functions—guiding their disciples and imparting the wisdom they have acquired over many years. The term "godfather" has an obvious derivation from gangster movies. Godfathers (sometimes called "rabbis") are in a position to intervene on your behalf; by definition, they are powerful people with an interest in your career.

How do mentors and godfathers differ? A major difference is that a godfather must be employed in the same company you are; mentors

CHART 7.1

MENTOR OR GODFATHER?

MENTOR	GODFATHER
• A mentor is someone who teaches you by example and direction. He or she helps you learn and frequently assists in problem solving.	• A godfather likes your style, skills, results, or is connected to you politically in some way. He or she helps your career from time to time and may be able to protect you in politically difficult situations.
• Can work anywhere or not work at all. Must have skills or knowledge to impart. Can be your boss or even a co-worker.	• Should work for the same company or agency you do; preferably *not* your boss. Must be higher than you in the organization.
• Must generate your respect and trust.	• Need not be someone you respect, but must be powerful or influential.
• Must have frequent contact with you.	• Doesn't require frequent contact but should be brought up to date periodically.

can be employed anywhere (or can be unemployed, retired, or self-employed). A mentor must be someone you trust; that trust is a basic requirement for the kind of exchange that takes place between you. A mentor will help you to learn and grow, sharing knowledge, experience (sometimes hard-won), and recommendations. The object is to help your career by making you a better manager.

A godfather (male or female*) is a person who helps promote your career within an organization. You needn't like or trust a godfather in order to have a mutually beneficial relationship. (You can even, although it's not recommended, blackmail someone into performing the duties of a godfather—protecting you in times of political trouble and

---

*Ah ... godperson? Yuk! One of the authors is female; one is male. We believe in equal rights, equal pay, and equal words, but enough is enough!

advancing your career when possible. It's not recommended for three reasons: one, it's unethical; two, it can backfire; three, you've just made a powerful enemy.)

How do you find a mentor? Just as you would find a friend. Notice those people whom you respect and who have skills or knowledge you would like to have. Pick someone you like, and someone who is busy. (Here, as elsewhere, a busy person is more likely to really be of help than the person who has lots of time.) Then just ask. Say something like "I really respect your skills as a manager and admire the way you handle people. May I ask you for help or feedback from time to time? I want to be a successful manager and would like you to be my mentor."

Locating a godfather is frequently less direct. If you are both good at your job and lucky (luck does play a part in any career), you may be fortunate enough to have a godfather select you. Notice those in your organization who are powerful. Take the risks associated with being visible (otherwise potential godfathers will never notice you). Make presentations to visiting managers, give tours of your area, volunteer to work on special projects. Then look around. Who's watching you? Make a note of those who are impressed or with whom you think you could work.

Unfortunately, while it is possible to ask someone to be your mentor, you can't ask someone to be your godfather. What you can do, however, is seize every opportunity to work with potential godfathers and impress them. To a large extent, the most powerful godfathers cannot be manipulated into becoming your patron and will probably be aware of any manipulating you try; after all, they didn't reach high positions in a company without being aware of what goes on around them.

It *is* possible to approach a potential godfather who is only a few levels above you. One type of godfather is the person who, while not in a powerful position, is a trusted assistant to someone who is powerful. Often this person will not be so senior to you as to be inaccessible. If other means fail, approach your potential godfather *as you would a mentor*. Ask for advice, impress him if you can, become part of his network. (Section III will discuss networks in detail.) If that fails, you have to go back to square one. Examine what you've done. Were you sufficiently impressive? Was your work of high caliber? Were you visible enough? If you weren't, correct the problem areas. If you were, look around to find another potential candidate.

If you are successful at attracting a godfather, make sure you stay visible. Depending on the conventions of your corporate culture, either call or write about every six months to keep him or her up to date on your progress. Unless you're very comfortable and friendly with your godfather, don't just say "hi." Find a business reason to get in touch. Certainly make him aware of any job changes; you can use the excuse of sending your new address and phone number.

Now That You've Hooked the Fish, Don't Lose It

Listed below are some quick, common-sense questions you can ask yourself to help you maintain a good relationship with your mentor or godfather.

1. Do I keep my mentor or godfather up to date? (Discuss your status with a mentor at least once a month. It is probably only necessary to discuss status with your godfather once every six months.)

2. Recognizing that my mentor or godfather has many other pressing responsibilities, am I careful not to drag or make unreasonable demands upon that person's time?

3. Do I thank him or her for the time and help invested in me? (Buying lunch or a drink, or sending a birthday or holiday card may be appropriate depending upon the type of relationship.)

4. Do I find ways to help my mentor or godfather?

5. Am I earning the information I receive by intelligently applying what I'm taught?

6. Although I am receiving help, do I remain independent as a manager?

7. Do I stay in contact with godfathers from previous firms?

If the answer to all these questions is yes, you are performing your part in the relationship. If not, and if you don't change your ways, it's likely that soon you won't *have* a relationship.

Mentors

Probably the most important thing a mentor can do is to provide you with patterns of successful behavior (through example or stories) in the areas you are learning. You can also use your mentor as a sounding board—preferably before you take action—discussing potential approaches to opportunities or solutions to problems. And even if you didn't use your mentor as a sounding board (or you did and it went sour anyway), your mentor can help you pick up the pieces and put the situation back on track. Don't be embarrassed to discuss failures with your mentor. You may even find that you learn more from your difficulties than from your successes. Besides your mentor can pat you on the back and help you return to a more positive frame of mind.

Aside from the more obvious benefits, you may find that your mentors become lifelong friends—enriching both of your lives. While generally beneficial, this relationship carries with it a hidden risk. As people grow at different rates, you may outgrow your mentors. Some mentors become quite parental, and it may be difficult to declare your independence without hurting a person who has given you so much help. (It is a problem similar to that which children, emerging into adulthood, have with their parents.) If you are much more successful than some of your early mentors, you may also be uncomfortable in their presence. They may ask for jobs or help you may be unable (or unwilling) to give. No single answer is the right one, but awareness and tact will help if these troubling situations should arise.

Finally you should be aware that sexual relationships frequently become a part of mentoring. Learning in an atmosphere of close and mutual trust is a natural for romance. However, surveys of both sides involved in successful mentor relationships indicate that even those who have been sexually involved recommend against it. Both mentors and proteges (mentees?) come to regret the sexual liaison at a later time. It tends to complicate the business relationship and to make declaring independence an even greater emotional wrench. Your choice: if you play, you pay.

Godfathers

As you are usually not as close personally to a godfather as you are to a mentor, neither the benefits nor the drawbacks of friendship apply. A godfather can help you to get promotions and make career moves and can sometimes help you get out of difficult political situations. In fact, if you are known to have a godfather, the political trouble often stops before it starts. It is easier to find other "prey." There are, however, two dangers from godfathers:

1. You can become too dependent, forcing you either to manage in

ways you would not choose on your own or to count on your godfather to do more than is possible.

2. You become so tied to your godfather that, if his or her star falls, you fall with it.

The solutions to these dangers are first, to be a competent manager in your own right; second, to have more than one godfather (or to be clairvoyant enough to pick one who never gets in trouble); and, third, to resist becoming dependent. Easier written than done, but a recognition of the problems may help.

Since it's been mentioned in relation to mentors, a word here about sex in a godfather relationship: don't. Most people in a corporation will accept, however reluctantly, promotions and recognition you receive that are partially the result of a godfather's intervention. As long as you are actually deserving of what you receive, it may generate envy but is unlikely to generate widespread hostility. If, however, there is even a rumor of a sexual liaison, you will find all your credit destroyed. No matter how well you do your job, you will be branded as having "slept your way to the top." In a recent case that made national headlines, a senior vice president (female) of a major multinational who had been promoted rapidly was forced to resign in the wake of allegations that she had been having an affair with the president of the company (male). Her resignation came not because the affair was revealed (it wasn't, both parties still deny it) nor because she was incompetent (some observers said she was, others said she wasn't). Her effectiveness as a manager was destroyed and her authority undermined by the allegations. She decided it was better to quit and start again elsewhere than to try to continue. No one, it seems, likes or respects a cheat, and receiving promotion as a result of a sexual relationship generates tremendous hostility and destroys respect. As this example shows, it isn't even necessary for there to be proof—the general acceptance by others that the allegations are true is enough. Since by definition a godfather is going to help your career, do your best to see that the relationship offers no fuel for corporate gossip.

Spreading the Wealth

Become a mentor or godfather yourself. As you succeed, your responsibility also grows. Having had the benefit of others' experience, it is time to share yours. Besides it's fun and it enhances your power and reputation. The time and effort you invest will be more than repaid by those you help. Your responsibilities include honesty (even when it's uncomfortable), sharing your knowledge and experiences, and, most important, taking an interest in and encouraging those who want to learn.

CHART 7.2

AN EXTENDED BUSINESS FAMILY

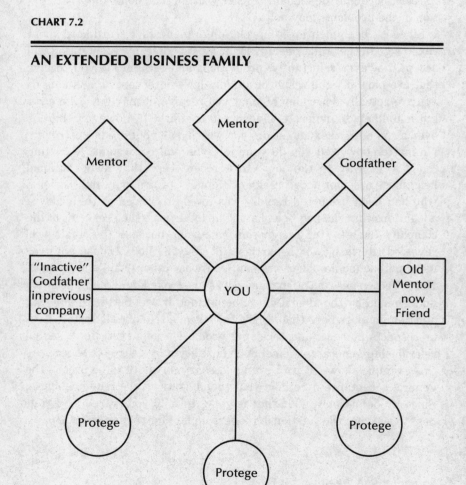

SECTION II

MANAGING DOWN

Introduction

Managing up can help your career significantly. Your job, however, does not stop there. The very fact that you are in (or want to be in) *middle* management implies that you manage staff who report to you, responding to the needs of your organization.

As a middle manager, you may have a staff of one or two or be in charge of a "body shop" of 50 or 100 people or more. Your staff may all be in the office right outside your door or scattered in separate locations all around the country—or around the world, with the attendant difficulties of different languages, different customs, and different time zones. Whatever your actual situation, it is your dealings with your subordinates that is usually called management. The most common definition of management is "getting things done through other people."

While there are as many different ways of managing as there are managers, certain general styles can be isolated. Attila the Hun was a manager—he didn't ravage Europe by himself; so was Thomas Jefferson, who was not only a politician but profitably managed Monticello, his Virginia plantation. They did not use the same management styles. More important, each had to deal with different types of employees and different objectives.

They did have something in common, however: the success of their enterprises depended on how their subordinates performed. No manager can do all the work without help—though some try. The only sure road to success as a middle manager is to develop and manage a staff capable of meeting the objectives set for your area on time and with consistently high quality.

A few years ago the words "the only sure road to success" would have been preposterous. Almost everything written about business included some techniques for manipulation and gamesmanship. Studies of success-ful executives (such as Michael Macoby's *The Gamesman*) showed that

"I give you weapons . . .
I give you horses . . .
I give you guidance . . .
What the hell is wrong with you guys!?"

those who got ahead were the ones who always put their own interests first, using people, especially those reporting to them, as means to further their own ends. Inevitably this one-sided pursuit of advancement meant neglecting the interests of subordinates and peers.

The Sixties and Seventies, however, were times of great social change, and business did not escape the effects of these changes. Events such as Watergate led to a reexamination of ethical standards; college students entering the business world brought with them some of the attitudes that sparked the campus rebellions. The new employees, from clerical help all the way to executive row, tended to show more independence and to be more resistant to coercion from above. Studies showed that even senior executives preferred more time off to more money.

Simultaneously, the scandals that rocked many major corporations in the late Seventies and early Eighties—bribery, hidden hazardous waste dumps, product recalls—discredited many executives of the gamesman type, removing them as successful role models. The combination of employees who refused to be pushed and the failure of many executives who had been pushers has led to drastic changes in management styles.

To be successful today's executive must manage with the help of his or her staff. To motivate today's work force—the best educated, least dependent work force ever—requires new techniques. The successful manager of today is a leader rather than a manipulator. (For more on this, see Maccoby's update on *The Gamesman*, entitled *The Leader*.) Good leaders develop successful teams of managers and supervisors reporting to them, fostering loyalty in the process. If you work hard at building a staff, you can become a successful leader.

This section will show you the techniques and shortcuts that will not only allow you to develop such a staff but also keep it running well despite the inevitable stresses and strains of the corporate environment.

8

Invest in Your Staff—
It's Like Money in the
Bank

Do you want power, fame, and riches? A good staff can help you get them. A good staff does not, however, spring full-grown from the forehead of Zeus, or ripen on trees for easy plucking. A staff must be built. You will probably be able to select only part of your staff. Your options are often limited; the selection may be narrowed by personnel or budgetary considerations, or you may have to use staff members who are already in place. Since usually you can't fire your entire staff and start over, the solution is to transform the current staff into an ideal one. Helping your staff members to learn and grow is, in effect, helping yourself.

You Can't Just Ask for a Bankbook—How Do You Invest in Your Staff?

Like everything else in management (in life?), you have to invest before you can reap rewards. Investing in people is like investing in the stock market or real estate: although it's tricky—each employee is unique after all—certain tested techniques should improve your success rate. Just as monetary investments require planning and daily monitoring, in order to invest successfully in your staff, you need a game plan. And you need to break down the game plan into steps that can be incorporated into your daily work schedule.

What goes into the plan? There are many options. You can invest in your staff members by:

- Teaching and coaching them on the job yourself
- Arranging for others to do the same
- Providing them with opportunities to experience different types of management situations and styles
- Enrolling them in formal training
- Encouraging formal education when appropriate (check your company's tuition refund plan)
- Giving them more responsibility in small pieces

Of course, the type and level of investment will be different for different levels of employees. You wouldn't ask a customer-service representative to represent you at a budget meeting; but neither should you ignore the chance to have that same representative present the new system to an executive vice president or to sit on a service-delivery panel. More senior personnel can be helped in the same way. Junior managers, for instances, can rotate handling your mail and "running" the office in your absence. It will give them a taste of responsibility and give *you* a chance to evaluate their corporate maturity and progress.

It Seems Like a Lot of Work. What's in It for Me?

Many managers make the mistake of only looking at short-term progress and think of staff development as a long-term (postponable) ideal. The time and effort a manager needs to develop a staff is often in short supply; and it is easy to say "I just don't have the time" or "I'm too busy on the ESP project to do any of that staff development stuff now." Yet the benefits can be short-term as well as long term.

Ask yourself the following questions:

1. Can you go on vacation for at least two weeks without leaving a phone number and return with all tasks on schedule?

2. If you get sick can at least one (and preferably several) members of your staff step in for you—even during budget planning or at special presentations?

3. Can you consistently delegate major portions of the projects assigned to you, AND can you use the material prepared by your staff members?

4. Do you ask staff members to attend meetings in your stead, AND do those staff members usually make the same decisions you would have made?

5. Are you able to communicate easily with your staff, depending on a shared understanding and approach?

Sound like a desirable situation for a manager? If you can answer these questions with a yes, you are already investing in your staff whether you realize it or not. If your answers included some "no's,"

CHART 8.1

THE BENEFITS OF INVESTING IN YOUR STAFF

A KNOWLEDGEABLE, SKILLED EMPLOYEE WHO KNOWS YOUR PHILOSOPHY CAN:	BENEFIT TO YOU:
• Accept and complete assignments with minimal direction.	• Frees you to manage and devote your time to planning ahead.
• Stand in for you at meetings.	• Allows you to "be in two places at the same time."
• Take over while you are on vacation.	• Gives you time to rest, relax, and have fun.
• Communicate quickly (almost in shorthand) with you.	• Once again, saves you time and effort. Makes your work relationship more pleasant (less stress and frustration on both sides).
• Make a good impression in meetings, formal or informal, while representing your area.	• What makes your department look good, makes you look good.

You may notice that a staff member in whom you have invested will probably begin to establish a working style with you—just as you have done with your manager. You can help that process. Use your staff to help you manage yourself.

then you need to do more. You will reap many benefits in addition to those above by investing in your staff. The most important benefits are:

● You are able to do your job well because you have the right support when you need it.

● You have time to relax.

● You have the satisfaction of knowing that your staff members are growing.

Some people may look askance at including satisfaction in a catalog of benefits. Don't. Anyone who has been a parent, teacher, or mentor has experienced the deep and lasting rewards of teaching. Literature is full of it: Shaw's *Pygmalion* (or its more recent musical version, *My Fair Lady*) is a classic example. You can have that kind of satisfaction, with the additional reward of helping yourself as well.

Note also that staff members whom you have developed and guided toward fulfilling and productive careers will tend to be loyal, even if they (or you) move on. They will talk about you positively, which will help your reputation; and they are likely to stay in touch, which will aid in gathering political information and corporate intelligence. They will, in short, be part of your network.

Pretty impressive, isn't it? Spend some time and work on your staff and you achieve three things: one, you help yourself look better in the short run and lessen your work load; two, you get the satisfaction of helping others and watching them grow; three, you add to your future political strength.

If All This Is True, Why Doesn't Everyone Invest in Staff Members?

There are lots of reasons why managers don't invest in those who report to them. Most of them fall into five areas.

REASON ONE:
Fear. Fear that knowledgeable employees will do better than the manager himself, or that knowledgeable employees will be less easy to control. Some managers are afraid to let their employees get close enough to see that management sometimes makes mistakes.

Fallacy: There are few companies in which you can be promoted without having a successor. In addition, most corporations reward those managers who successfully develop other managers. (Some companies even make the career development of subordinates a key part of all managers' objectives.) Just because an employee *can* do your job doesn't mean you automatically lose it. There are many more people capable of senior management than actual positions. If an employee is brighter or a better leader than you are, holding back information will only cause that employee to seek it elsewhere. Your management control will only be further weakened. Intimidating employees through fear and lack of knowledge does work in some cases, but it requires constant attention and force. It also builds up considerable resentment. You can control a prisoner with guns, guards, and bars—but you must always have the restraints. You can manage someone you trust by explaining the rules and asking for cooperation—much less effort in the long run.

REASON TWO:

Lack of time—yours or your employees'.

Fallacy: Everyone has time pressures. But if you don't invest time and effort in developing knowledgeable employees, you'll *always* have time pressures. The person who must do everything herself is not a good manager and will ultimately fail.

You are fooling yourself if you say you don't have the time. Make time, even if it is only 15 minutes a day. If you can't find 15 minutes per day, you're in real trouble and shouldn't have time to be reading this. Fifteen minutes per day for three months (working days only) is 15 hours—the equivalent of many college-course classroom hours. If you don't think you have enough time for investing in your staff, you are probably procrastinating!

REASON THREE:

Lack of understanding of the value of a well-trained and informed staff.

Fallacy: You no longer have this excuse. Look at the reasons listed above to refresh your memory when necessary.

REASON FOUR:

Belief that his or her staff members can't be or aren't motivated to learn more senior tasks.

Fallacy: In some (very, *very* few) cases, this may be true. More often it is a management excuse. Don't believe it until you've honestly given it your best shot for at least three months. Even the most apparently unproductive employee magically springs to life when given the chance to learn new things and make a real contribution.

REASON FIVE:

Lack of skills necessary to develop immediate staff. You may know how to do the job but be unable to teach someone else how to do it.

Fallacy: If you can do the job and you are capable of managing a staff, you have two of the four ingredients necessary: you know how to perform the specific tasks, and you have some communication skills. You will also need patience (a matter of personal discipline and a few tricks listed in chart 8.2) and an on-the-job-training technique. The training technique is discussed in Chapter 9.

One note of warning: don't abuse your staff in the name of developing them. If you are really sick during the budget cycle, that's one thing; on the other hand, it is entirely unfair to dump your responsibility on an inadequately prepared employee so that you can play.

CHART 8.2

TRICKS OF PATIENCE

1. Say something good about an employee you are speaking with before saying something bad. The effort will tend to calm you down before reaching the stressful remarks *and* you will lighten the atmosphere for both of you—avoiding conflict.

"Your work has really improved lately, John. I'm very pleased. There's one area that still needs attention, though. . . ."

2. Wait until next time to criticize. (Don't start a critique while you're angry.)

3. Think about the last time *you* made a big mistake or just couldn't understand a new concept before you meet with an errant employee. How did you feel? Keep it in mind and you are more likely to give constructive, understanding criticism that will help the employee rather than just let you blow off steam.

4. Don't expect perfection the first, second, or even third try.

5. Try to do teaching and coaching when you're in a good mood—and when there is little time pressure.

Employees will quickly catch on, your relationship with them will deteriorate, and they will either stop producing or deliberately sabotage you. It's not worth it. Investing in your staff does not include delegating all the dirty work.

Make the effort and you will quickly see the results. Your job will be easier and your staff will work better. Best of all, you will soon be in a position to move onwards and upwards because your department will be producing quality work, enhancing *your* reputation, and because you will already have developed your replacement. Don't wait; start now.

9

Winners: How to Hire and Develop Your Team

Picture yourself in this situation: you are sitting in your new office, in surroundings that indicate you have finally arrived in upper-middle management. On the desk in front of you is a sheet of paper labeled "Objectives." Outside the desks where your staff will sit are empty. No one is making coffee in the brand new coffee-machine. No one sits at the secretary's desk outside your door. The department is empty.

The first major objective assigned to you by your new boss is due in four months. Between now and then you must not only perform well—you have to justify your promotion—but also must hire and train a staff. The department you have been promoted to head is a new one. You have only an incomplete list of positions to fill and the salary guidelines laid down by your boss. What do you do first? (Besides have a nervous breakdown, that is.)

In the Beginning, There Were—or Should Have Been—Job Descriptions

When was the last time you looked at your employees' job descriptions? (You may find your chief supervisor's position description includes filling the coal stove and lighting the oil lamps.) How about your own? Chances are you haven't looked at them recently—or, if you have, that you discovered they were woefully out of date. Kept up to date and *used*, they can become the key to building an effective team.

You can use job descriptions for many purposes, rewriting them for specific uses as appropriate. Use position descriptions to:

- *Recruit new staff members*
  A clear job description will help you to advertise correctly and will give applicants a clear idea of what skills are needed.
- *Determine the level and salary of a position*
  This is the official version of the position—the one personnel and compensation use to evaluate the job and to assign salary and status levels. Many managers artificially enhance jobs in order to obtain better salaries for their staff members. While not generally a good practice (outright lying rarely is), it may sometimes be necessary to do this in order to reward your staff *equally*. Make sure you can defend what you write and be careful never to get your staff ahead of parallel positions in the organization. It makes transfers and relocation next to impossible. Being overpaid is not a joke.
- *Help you organize the staff reporting to you effectively*
  After all, you, the company, and your employees must have a common idea of what is to be happening. Job descriptions help you to set up a smoothly functioning team with no duplication of effort. Along with mutually determined goals, a thoughtfully prepared description can become an informal contract between you and your employees. Especially effective with career-oriented supervisors and managers, you can balance unpleasant requirements with opportunities for new responsibilities or expanded scope. (In many countries, it also serves as a legal employment contract.)

If you don't have job descriptions, or they aren't current or effective, promptly start to create them. A good job description begins with a general statement of the purpose of the position (sometimes called a mission) followed by an indication of scope. Then come the details: list the specific tasks the employee performs and give the percentage of the total job time devoted to each task; enumerate the staff (with direct and indirect reporting relationships), budget, equipment and facilities, products, services, and projects for which the employee is responsible; write down the amount of executive or customer contact the person in this position has within and outside the company; finally, draw an organization chart showing at least two positions above and below the position. See chart 9.1 for an example of a completed job description.

CHART 9.1

A SAMPLE JOB DESCRIPTION

 INFERNAL INDUSTRIES, LTD.
"Our Aim is to Please"

JOB DESCRIPTION:
SCREWTAPE—Senior Devil

MISSION___To carry out the organization's objectives pertaining to temptation and soul collection

SCOPE___Western Europe, North Atlantic, North America east of Mississippi—All Souls resident

Major Tasks:	Percentage of Time:
1. Supervision of subordinates & overseeing of their work (other than (6) below)	35%
2. Membership in policy committee setting regional goals	15%
3. Training of subordinates (items not-delegatable)	5%
4. Direct temptation (major personalities only)	15%
5. Collection (major personalities only)	5%
6. Fulfilling sales contracts (including direct supervision of subordinates) (major personalities only)	25%

CHART 9.1 (Continued)

RESPONSIBILITIES

Staff Management:

Directly _5 executives, 15 managers, 500 demons, 800 imps_ Number __1320__

Indirectly _1 executive (detached to Trans-Mississippi)_ Number __2__
1 executive (Rock-stars—roving)

Budget Managed: Expense __$15.5 Billion__

Assets __$125 Billion__

Profit __12,500 Souls/M__

Equipment: _See list attached_

Facilities: _See list attached_

Products or Services: _Love, money, power, sex, health, wisdom, revenge_

Amount of Internal Contact:

Staff __minimal__

Management __extensive__

Amount of External Contact:

Customers __150MM__

Vendors __15,000__

Other __75 (writers)__

CHART 9.1 (Continued)

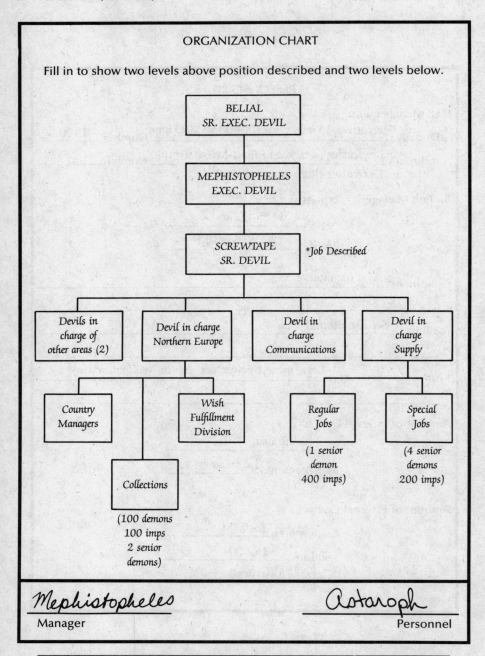

ORGANIZATION CHART

Fill in to show two levels above position described and two levels below.

BELIAL
SR. EXEC. DEVIL

MEPHISTOPHELES
EXEC. DEVIL

SCREWTAPE
SR. DEVIL   *Job Described

- Devils in charge of other areas (2)
- Devil in charge Northern Europe
- Devil in charge Communications
- Devil in charge Supply

Country Managers

Wish Fulfillment Division

Regular Jobs
(1 senior demon 400 imps)

Special Jobs
(4 senior demons 200 imps)

Collections
(100 demons
100 imps
2 senior
demons)

Mephistopheles
Manager

Astaroph
Personnel

Unless you are participating in a start-up and have no incumbents, always ask the person currently holding the job to do a separate analysis indicating the different types of tasks completed and the amount of time spent on each. He or she may list tasks you have forgotten or never even knew about, or you may find that staff members are duplicating each other's efforts or wasting time doing uneeded work. You can always mold or change the official nature of the job after you have considered all of the data. A more efficient team sends everyone home sooner and creates a better working environment. (By the way, this is an interesting thing for you to do with your own job description. You may find yourself redirecting your own energies as well.)

After you've written the first draft, leave it for a day or two, then review it carefully before considering it final. Think about how this position relates to others in your shop. Have you just inserted a quill-pen pusher into the middle of a computerized network? The structure of your organization can cost you continuing inefficiencies and internal political hassles or can send you home whistling early on Friday afternoons.

New Blood! How to Get the Best

Hiring can be lots of fun and very satisfying. You get to meet interesting people, and you have the opportunity to add to your team a person of your choosing. However, not everyone agrees on the type of person which should be hired to fill any particular position. (Did you ever wonder who hired some of the clods you have to work with now?) The hiring process is really like any other management process: the better the planning you do, the more likely you are to succeed.

Step 1

Get all of your ducks in line before you start. Begin by setting up the job within the context of your current organization. Prepare the job description, modifying it for different purposes. Then validate or revalidate the position title, grade, and salary (or salary range) through personnel. Prepare the personnel requisition making sure to define the specific reasons for filling this position, and get management approval to hire a person with the specified qualifications at the specified grade and salary. Do NOT start without this approval. You may be wasting your time.

Step 2

Use the position description to develop recruiting ads, an internal job posting, or whatever other means are available for recruitment. Be sure to list the experience needed. Currently in some areas of business an unwarranted emphasis is placed on education. While education certainly never hurt anyone, business experience with proven results may be more useful. Consider it carefully before you stipulate the minimum requirements. You may wish to use a listing similar to this: "College degree or equivalent business experience preferred."

Step 3

Establish a system to track all applicants. (Chart 9.2 is an example of such a record.) It is unbelievably rude and, at the very least, a poor business practice not to write a short note of rejection to all unsuccessful applicants. Prepare files to keep track of résumés in various stages (for example, not qualified, interviewed and rejected, second interview, etc.). Your secretary can be a great help if you include him in the process.

Step 4

Prepare yourself for the interview. Begin by thinking about the skills and personal attributes of those who have been successful in the job. Put together an interviewing package which includes a job description, an organization chart showing this job in relation to others, some samples of the work to be performed, and anything else that might be appropriate. Have copies of your annual report or other descriptive brochures available for interviewees.

CHART 9.2

HIRING RECORD

HIRING RECORD

POSITION TO BE FILLED: TELEPHONE SUPERVISOR

CANDIDATE'S NAME	SALARY REQUIREMENTS	RESUME SCREENING ACCEPTED/REJECTED	PERSONNEL PRESCREEN INTERVIEW	ACCEPTED/REJECTED	NOTES	INTERVIEW NOTES	REFERENCE CHECK	ACCEPTED/REJ.
Eager Beaver	$40-$45M	A	P. Player	A	- Good comm. skills - High energy	- Rolm & Collins Exp. - Budget $1 mm - 100+ staff	✓	A
Delightful Dahlia	$35M+	A	P. Player	A?	- Enthusiastic - Background light?	- Rolm Exp. - Budget $.5M? - 80+ staff		R

SECOND INTERVIEWER'S NAME	SECOND INTERVIEW NOTES	ACCEPTED/REJECTED	HIRE? YES	NO	CANDIDATE'S RESPONSE	ADDITIONAL NOTES
A. Arondale	- Strong candidate - Needs more info on benefits	A				

Write down some standard questions that you will ask all applicants (so that you have a basis for comparisons). Some of your questions should be skill-and-results oriented. For example: "Tell me about a situation where you wanted to implement a program or project and there was resistance from your management or peers. What skills did you use and what was the result?" For a college student with little work experience, you might ask: "How and why did you select the college you attended? The electives you took?" Ask open-ended questions (questions that can't be answered with "yes" or "no") whenever possible as you will learn more about how the candidate thinks. You are also less likely to give away the "right" answer. Always ask why the applicant chose to apply for this position and, towards the end of the interview, why you should hire this person over all the others you interviewed. A useful question to ask at the conclusion is "Is there anything else I should know about you?" (See Chart 9.3 for some sample questions.)

If at all possible, develop a short skills demonstration (test) each applicant can take. For your secretary, a dictation and typing test may be in order. For supervisors, you might ask for a short writing sample. Since the test is administered under your auspices, you will learn whether, for example, all of the writing samples presented by the candidate were edited (or prepared!) by someone else. As long as they are directly applicable to the job for which you are hiring, tests will help you defend yourself in case a disgruntled applicant sues you. Demonstrations of skill will also help you sell your candidate to management.

Step 5

Enlist the help of the personnel department and several of your peers or subordinates. If possible arrange to have personnel prescreen your applicants. Then each clerical applicant should be interviewed by two people and each management candidate by at least three. Particularly in the management area, you are looking not only for the right skills but also for the right chemistry. Will your applicant work well with other players already on board? Be sure to explain the nuances of what you are looking for before the interviewing starts.

It would take an entire book to cover the art of interviewing in depth. (If you need help in this area, there are specialized books on the subject available in most bookstores.) Chart 9.4 lists the basic struc-

CHART 9.3

SAMPLE INTERVIEW QUESTIONS AND TOPICS

- What do you like most (and least) about your current job?

- How would your current employer (or most recent professor or teacher) evaluate your performance? Do you agree? Why? Have you ever been rated below standard? Why?

- When was the last time you helped a peer to do something that wasn't strictly your job? What did you do? Why?

- What do you consider the most important decision (or sale or solution to a problem) you made during your career to date? What did you do to make it happen? Why?

- Tell me about a time when you had to change direction? What did you do?

- Be sure to ask some skill-related questions. You will have to design these based on the position for which you are hiring. Two examples are:
  For a Telephone Center Supervisor:
  —Which system of call handling and distribution do you favor? Why?
  For a Training Instructor:
  —How would you begin to design a course on basic accounting?

- Be sure to explain all of the job requirements—especially those that might be considered negatives (some examples are long hours, high pressure, travel, evaluation techniques). Then ask directly: Is there any part that you cannot do or that makes you feel uncomfortable?

- Understanding that most people would like to have a large office, lots of power, an impressive title, and make a million dollars a year, what compensation and rewards are most important to you?

- Tell me about the time during your career (schooling) that you were most unhappy. What factors made you uncomfortable?

- What would you like to be doing at work in five years? (Don't look for a title; look for type and amount of responsibility.)

- What do you do when you're not working?

ture of an hour-long interview. Don't neglect the portion of the interview in which you thoroughly describe the job. After describing the job, listen to the types of questions a candidate asks. The things that a person asks about will give you some idea of what he or she values. Take notes. If you interview more than five people, you begin to forget whether it was Svelte Susan or Dirty Harry that impressed

CHART 9.4

STRUCTURING THE SELECTION INTERVIEW

STEP	TIME ALLOTTED
I. BEFORE THE INTERVIEW	
—Review what you know about the candidate (from résumé, references, etc.) —Review your needs (what skills, etc. are needed for the position to be filled) —Review what questions you are going to ask the candidate	
II. THE INTERVIEW	60 minutes total
1. Introduction: —Introduce yourself —Put the candidate at ease —Review the job briefly —Review the structure of the interview	5 minutes
2. Ask the candidate questions, including: —background —skills —results achieved in previous jobs —strengths/weaknesses for position in question	20 minutes
3. Review the job in greater detail using: —job description —work samples —job aids	10 minutes
4. The candidate asks you questions about: —position —company —benefits* It is not necessary to give a candidate a specific salary figure until you are ready to make an offer.	10 minutes

*This assumes that the candidate *will* ask questions. Not all candidates will, for any of a variety of reasons: nervousness, ignorance, etc. One of the judgment calls you must make is whether or not to help the candidate at this point (by prompting, for instance) and whether the position is such that the lack of questions on the candidate's part should be considered a strike against the candidate.

5.	Ask the candidate further questions based on the interview thus far	10 minutes

6.	Close the interview. Be sure to:	5 minutes
	—ask for any further information you need (such as references)	
	—give the candidate an approximate time frame for the hiring decision	

III. AFTER THE INTERVIEW

—Have the candidate take a skills test
—Expand on your notes while they're fresh

you with a new approach to systems design. A selection interview should be a two-way process. If a candidate doesn't want the job, you shouldn't hire that person. In the end turnover is much more expensive than an extended search.

Even if pressed for time no interview should be less than an hour; the result will be frustration and eventually a poor decision. Especially if you are pressured take a moment to relax before you begin. (Consulting your prepared list of questions will help you to get started or put you back on track if you get distracted during the interview.) The major points to remember are (1) you control the process (an easy way to establish control is to outline the hour at the beginning of the interview); (2) you should focus your attention in every way possible on the individual you are interviewing (observe dress, mannerisms, and body language; listen carefully not only to the words but also to the intent behind the words); and (3) you should avoid for as long as possible (several months perhaps) hiring a compromise candidate (just the right candidate is out there somewhere!).

Studies have shown that many interviewers make up their minds about a candidate within the first five minutes of the interview. Guard against this tendency. You could lose a candidate with outstanding potential simply because he or she was too nervous to warm up in the first few minutes.

Speaking strategically, it is best to select three candidates for each position before you make your presentation to management. If, for any reason, senior management should reject your leading candidate, you have two others to choose from without starting over. Present the leading candidate as if you were selling—because you are. Lead off (either orally or in writing) with his or her strengths; counter any possible objections. However, don't list them as objections, simply include them as a part of the candidate's background.

Don't cut corners: you're going to have to live with whomever you hire for a long time.

Whatever Else You May Do, You Never Get the Chance to Welcome and Orient an Employee after the First Day

Now that you've hired the best, don't ruin your coup. Lenin was quite right when he said "give me a child and he's mine forever." Although you won't be hiring children, your employees will remember their first day on the job. It sets the tone and is particularly important in service industries. Employees tend to treat customers the way they have been treated. If you plan to demand a lot from your staff members, give them a first-class welcome.

Even under the most difficult circumstances, you can have the employee's new or temporary desk ready for occupancy with a bare minimum of a pen, pad, internal telephone directory, an organization directory, and some reading material about the new job. It would also be nice to have a note of welcome, a name plate, and, perhaps, an office plant.

If your company has an orientation program, learn all about it and let your newly hired employee know what to expect. Arrange to provide any of the following that are not included (or if there is no formal orientation program, arrange for all of them):

- A review of the overall company, the division, and the department in which the employee will be working

- The details of when and how the employee will be paid (it's amazing how often this isn't done)

- The standards the employee is expected to meet and the ways in which he or she will be measured

- A tour of the facility in which the employee will be working, including places to park, eat lunch, take breaks, etc.

Add whatever other information is needed and assign the new employee a buddy from the ranks of your current staff who can help smooth the introductions and learning process. Whatever temporary time or productivity loss that results will be more than compensated for by a new employee who feels at home from the start. If you demand the best, you must provide the best you can in the way of support.

Coaching: The Means to Develop Winners

It is the last quarter of the game, the score is 14-14, the ball on the 50-yard line. The clock is ticking down the final seconds. The quarter-back fades back; the opposing linemen close in from both sides. He fires a short pass straight into the arms of his tight end. The receiver tucks the ball firmly into the crook of his arm just as he is hit hard by an opposing tackle. He staggers but miraculously keeps his feet and holds on to the ball. An offensive lineman takes out the tackle before he can hit again. For a heart-stopping moment the dazed receiver is alone. He shakes his head, realizes there is no defender between him and the goal line, and takes off. Thousands of people come to their feet screaming. Dimly, still shaken by the collison, the receiver catches a glimpse of his teammates grappling with the opposing team. The goal line is just ahead. With a final burst of effort, he crosses the line, the adrenaline pumping through his system. Elated, he spikes the ball, leaping high into the air. His teammates rush up to him. Grinning, he raises his hands in victory. Then, gradually, as he sees the expressions on his teammates faces, he realizes something is wrong. He looks around. He has run the ball 56 yards over his own goal line.

It is an unusual but not unknown event for a football player to become disoriented and run towards the wrong goal. Humorous films of football mistakes often record these incidents, perhaps the most famous of which took place years ago during the Rose Bowl game. Target disorientation is, of course, not restricted to football. In fact, football coaches (and other sports coaches) are lucky; they have a clearly defined goal for their players. That's why target disorientation is unusual in sports. Off the playing field, however, direction is often harder to find, the well-defined goal is illusive, and target disorientation is a way of life.

Just because you don't have a clear goal marked by large posts at one end of a restricted field, however, doesn't mean you must muddle along without a sense of purpose. By understanding the goals yourself, presenting them properly to your staff, and following up in a timely manner, you can see to it that your people are at least running in the right direction.

CHART 9.5

GOALS

Your subordinate managers' and supervisors' goals should include at least one objective in each of the following areas:

- Financial
- Quality
- Creative
- Development of Staff
- Career
- Personal Development
- Major Project

Staff members (generally employees who are not exempt from Federal wage and salary laws—sometimes called nonexempt) should have the following types of objectives. Except for personal goals, you should set the same objectives—sometimes called standards—for all employees who perform the same job.

- Productivity
- Quality
- Timeliness
- Personal Development
- Career

Note: the career goal for any employee, whether manager, supervisor, or staff member, may be simply to remain in the same or equivalent position. It is *not* a necessity that all employees, even managers, seek to advance, provided they perform well. On the other hand, longevity in a position is no excuse for poor performance.

In most companies, there are three styles of goal setting: mandated goals (you and your employees are given goals with no discussion permitted); participative goals (you and your employees contribute to the goal-setting process but someone else makes the final decision); and individually determined goals (you and your employees set your goals with management concurrence). In any case, your goals should be well balanced. When you are preparing objectives with your financial analyst, be sure that he or she has more than just financial goals. (Chart 9.5 has some suggestions.) Without this balancing, you will create employees who are good at only one specialty and who cannot perform general management tasks. (Timothy Terrific, the Nobel Prize–winning research chemist who develops a cure for a different disease every year but is unable to do a performance appraisal, can't be promoted from the laboratory to manager of new product development.) Goals should have enough "stretch" to provide an interesting challenge, but they do a disservice to everyone if they are unreachable.

Whichever system your organization uses, make the process of goal setting a time to increase communication between you and your employees. If your staff can't participate in determining the objectives, they can still help to determine the methods that will be used to reach them. The more you can get your employees to participate, the more they will be involved and committed.

There is, of course, a difference between getting the 400 customer-service representatives who report to you to answer the phones with "Southeastern Polyester Growers' Cooperative, the home of organically grown plastic; may I help you?" and sitting down with the telecommunications manager to review her quarterly targets. Nonetheless, whether setting individual or group goals, you can use the same steps in holding a goal setting session:

- Give an overall review of the organization, its major objectives, and the part you and your employees play in reaching those objectives

- Review mandated goals or jointly set participative goals that line up with the organization

- Establish ways of meeting the goals by asking your employees *first*, then adding your own thoughts

- State your own commitment to the new goals and ask your employees to join with you in that commitment

- Set up regular ways of establishing that you are on target. (This may be a monthly status check with your subordinate managers or a chart posted in the telephone center listing the weekly monitoring scores.)

Making Sure Your Staff Is Running in the Right Direction

Once you have set goals with your employees, you must be sure to keep the lines of communication open. Since your ability to make decisions depends upon having correct information, really listen to what your employees tell you, and don't punish those who bring you honest information. If you shoot the messenger for telling you your favorite project isn't working, pretty soon your staff will tell you only what you want to hear—whether it is the truth or not. It's far better to hear the bad news from your subordinates—while you have time to do something about it—than from your boss when it's too late.

In addition to making sure that you keep the lines of communication open, you should observe your employees' performance both formally and informally. Informal observation is often simply a matter of being around and paying attention to what is going on, listening to your employees, and observing their work in the course of your daily routine. If your routine does not call for constant contact, develop one that does. Make it a habit to walk through the areas you supervise once a day if they are close at hand. That way you'll notice that the plastic parsley was left off the dinner plates before they reach the main dining room, and you'll be able to reestablish your standards before you lose all of your business to the diner across the street.

If you manage areas that are more than a short drive away, you will need to set up scheduled telephone calls and regular visits. You might plan to speak regularly with your senior manager in Boise every Tuesday night for at least 30 minutes. While you chat you can have a relaxed discussion that floats in and out of business and also includes the latest movies, sports scores, upcoming performance appraisals, your kids' performance in school, quality-control problems, and weekend plans. It isn't the same as a drink after work, but it can help to give you a better feel for what is happening in remote locations. The rapport you establish during these phone conversations will stand you in good stead when you must solve serious problems over the phone. Here, as in person, frequent contact does three things: (1) gives you a good rapport with your staff (you're not just someone who shows up when something is wrong), (2) helps you to have a better feel for what is really going on (which prevents disastrous surprises), and (3) enables your subordinates to learn from you.

During in-person informal observation be sure to reinforce positive behavior and to be friendly. Take note of problems you wish to address, but wait until another time to handle them. If a problem is so serious that an immediate correction is called for, remember to reprimand employees in private.

Sometimes an incident will make you want to strangle an employee. Refrain. Murder is bad for morale, and you'll never get all of your MBOs completed from jail. Try instead to understand why the idiot . . . ah, employee did what he did. Then try to make your correction constructive. If your senior manager takes three months of records home to work on over a weekend and loses them because her car is broken into, you may want to wait a while before writing a general memo instituting a new rule that documents must be duplicated before removing them from the building. Whether you choose this or another solution, don't punish a subordinate for putting in extra time. When possible, don't point fingers. The guilty will know who they are.

You should also observe your employees formally at least once a month. You may schedule a formal observation for a specific time or simply inform subordinates of your plans generally. For example, you might ask a subordinate supervisor to notify you of the next performance appraisal he will be doing so that you can sit in to observe his technique (specific), or you might say that you will be attending one of his weekly staff meetings in the next month (general).

During a formal observation take notes. Be sure to record specific examples of both positive and negative behavior. Immediately after your observation meet with the staff member. Review the entire task you observed. Start with the areas handled at or above standard. It is especially important to comment on the progress made since your last observation. This reinforces the new behavior and gives the employee a feeling of success which makes him or her more willing to try other new techniques—and to accept criticism without resentment.

Coaching and employee development is a continuous process. After each achivement, there are new goals to be set and a whole new cycle begins.

Developing a subordinate manager or supervisor is much like a coach developing an athlete. You correct, cajole, and comfort. Mostly you help—sometimes by leading and sometimes by pushing—your subordinate to learn, to grow, and to do his or her best. Remember your first budget presentation, the first time you fired someone, the first time your product outsold your predictions and ran out of stock? If you had a good manager who was also a leader you probably got through those events without undue difficulty. If not, you probably still have mental scars. Your job in developing your subordinates is to smooth the path, to share your knowledge, and to pick them up and brush them off when they trip. Set the stage correctly. It is much harder for your staff to try something new if they don't understand the benefits of the new skill. Any time that you ask an employee to try a new technique or learn a new skill, be sure to give the employee the requisite authority and support. And always remember that it is almost impossible to learn without making mistakes. If you punish a subordinate for making mistakes while learning, the employee is less likely to try new behavior or to take risks in the future.

Education and Training

Both education (the teaching of general knowledge; schooling as we normally think of it) and training (the teaching of specific skills; more often offered in corporations or for certification) are helpful to your subordinates during the development process.

A basic education including effective reading, clear writing, and basic math and statistics are necessary for every manager. Computer literacy is also far along the way to being essential. By all means encourage your employees to pursue an education—especially if it is remedial in nature—but always be careful that additional education doesn't get in the way of good business experience.

Training is the teaching of specific skills. It should result in the employee having the ability to *do* something he or she could not do before. You should take advantage of the very good training available in many companies. (Unfortunately, it *isn't* always good. Check with other managers who have used the programs before enrolling your employees.) There are also an increasingly large number of courses offered by colleges, consultants, and other businesses. Your corporate training department, the American Management Association, or your local business club should be able to recommend appropriate courses. In order to recoup your investment (in terms of expense and time), be

CHART 9.6

MAKING TRAINING WORK

To get maximum advantage from employee training courses, you must both prepare the employee before the course and follow up afterwards. Otherwise, the benefits of the training may be minimal or transitory.

WHEN TO DO IT	WHAT TO DO
1. **Some time before employee goes to course.**	Review: —course subject matter and reasons why employee is going. —your expectations. —timing. —location.
2. **Just before employee goes to course.**	Review: —course in detail. —what employee expects from course. —changes *you* expect in employee.
3. **During the course.**	Remove all duties from employee to allow concentration on course. If student/employee is a manager or supervisor, formally appoint someone to temporarily take over the student's supervisory tasks. Speak to student at least once during the course—but don't interrupt the class. Set up appointment for review on employee's return.
4. **After employee's return from course.**	Interview employee. —Review what was good and bad about course. —Agree on implementation of new knowledge and changes in behavior. —Set up regular follow-ups; be sure to enforce periodically. Set up presentation for employee to share new insights with peers if appropriate. Put a record in employee's file. (Files should always include good as well as bad.) Plan next stage of development. Recommend that others do/don't attend.

sure that the course you select directly applies to the skills needed on the job by your employee. Then coach the employee on what is expected and be sure to reinforce the new skills when the employee returns. Chart 9.6 lists these steps in greater detail.

O-J-T

In some cases (usually when the application of the skill is specific to your company or department), you will find it necessary to do some on-the-job training yourself. On-the-job training may be very beneficial to you despite the time it takes to prepare. You may learn a lot yourself— you have to know much more about a task in order to teach it well than is usually necessary to perform it.

- The first thing you *must* do is prepare yourself thoroughly, both in the knowledge of how to do the task you are going to teach and in the way you will teach it. Do all of the following that are practical:
  1. practice
  2. take notes
  3. get details and examples
  4. prepare job aids (Job aids are any easy reference materials an employee can keep at the workplace.)

- Next get together with the employee and explain what the task is. Beginning with an overview, give the employee a good picture of how, why, and where the task exists in the job flow (how it relates to the jobs of others). Explain what you will be teaching.

- Do the task yourself, explaining as you go. If for some reason you can't do the entire task, do at least a portion of it or show the employee examples. Ask for questions. Repeat the essential points until you are sure the employee understands. Then give the employee the job aids you have prepared or procured.

- Now have the employee demonstrate the new skills. Make any corrections that are needed. Review the task in isolation and then, once again, review it in relation to other jobs and the flow of tasks in the workplace.

- Finally, follow up. Watch for samples of the employee's work. Stop by several times and answer any additional questions. Comment favorably whenever possible. Work out any continuing problems.

A Short Note on a Rewarding but Very Difficult Technique

Listening—real listening—is deceptively hard. When you are listening to a staff member, focus your attention on that person. Watch his or her body language and facial expression. Think about what the person is saying—not what you will say in return. It isn't easy or everyone would do it. (How many people really listen to you?)

Once you have learned how to listen, practice it. You will find that this simple act will reward you with continuing dividends.

10

You Can Lead a Horse to Water, but . . . Motivating Your Staff

Okay, you've put together a great team and you're ready to take on the world, right? Wrong. A team composed of the right people, with the right training—even supported by your superior management—is still only *potentially* great. You still have to help that team work at its full potential.

You do that by helping your staff members to *want* to work hard, to go the extra mile. As a manager, you have many different tools available to create that special thing, a motivated staff. Many of these tools are obvious; some are often overlooked or misused.

Recognition: The Key to Employee Excellence

A senior vice president of a multinational corporation still remembers the award he won in the fifth grade for a poster he drew. The best part, he will tell you, was not the award itself—which was a fancy certificate—but the fact that it was given out during assembly in front of the whole school. That's recognition with a bang and he'll remember it all his life.

What makes someone want to do something? You can coerce people into doing things but that takes continual effort; as soon as you stop coercing, people stop working. Most successful managers today believe that people want to work and want to do well. Obviously it will be easier for *you* if you can somehow inspire people to want to do well. Lots of time and research has gone into the study of human psychology in the work place. According to Abraham Maslow, all human beings are motivated by the need or desire for five types of things:

1. Food and shelter
2. Security (food and shelter for tomorrow and next year)
3. Social acceptance (friends and family to laugh with, belong to, and depend upon)
4. Status (rank and power: not just the Rolls-Royce and the special parking space for it, but the authority to manage others)
5. Achievement (designing a system or painting a painting: accomplishing something of value to the individual whether or not anyone else likes it or even knows about it)

Everyone has most of these needs at one time or another, and you may have more than one at a time. People generally try to fill these needs in order. The senior vice president who won the award for his poster already had the first three levels of need filled when he achieved status by receiving an award in front of his classmates. Another senior executive in the same firm remembers a very bountiful Thanksgiving dinner at the same age. His family were migrant farm workers, and they were frequently hungry. An award for a poster—could he have imagined such a thing—wouldn't have interested him much. Now a very successful executive, he can afford to be interested in status and accomplishment.

How does this information help you to get better performance from your employees? If you understand what motivates your staff, you can better reward hard work and inspire even further accomplishments. Chart 10.1 summarizes some of the actions you may wish to take. You may not control all the factors affecting your staff—for example, few middle managers really influence the benefits packages offered by their organizations and they may be unable to determine pay grades— but you should fight as hard as you can within the system for your staff. If you don't work for them, why should they work for you?

CHART 10.1

MOTIVATING YOUR STAFF

NEED	WAYS TO SATISFY
1. Food and shelter	• Pay fairly. • To the best of your ability, provide a safe, comfortable place to work. • Make sure there is a convenient place for your employees to eat and relax.
2. Security	• Don't fire without warning *and* explain your actions (briefly) to the rest of your staff members. • If your organization offers benefits, be sure you understand them and can explain and administer them. • Make sure that staff members can bring their problems to you and that you settle them as fairly as possible.
3. Social Acceptance	• Build a team which includes everyone. • Be personally friendly or affectionate (but not parental) and interested (genuine or otherwise) in your employee's lives. • Settle disputes directly with the parties involved.
4. Status	• Base salary increases and promotions on merit and abilities. • Reward publicly; reprimand privately. • Share departmental and personal successes. Give credit where it is due. • Be sure to submit candidates from your area for all corporate recognition programs. • Develop your own symbols of achievement and award programs.
5. Achievement	• Take chances on people—give them new responsibilities and authority. • Arrange for training in new skills or do it yourself on the job. • Let your supervisors and managers do their jobs. (You do yours—which does *not* include overmanaging them.)

Creative Rewards

Money, unless you can give salary increases every week, can't be the only thing you use to motivate employees. (But do be careful to see that paychecks are on time and correct. If there is a problem, *you* fix it. Don't ask your employees to do so.) Creative rewards, then, are in order. For example, take a supervisor who has been asked to take on special additional assignments to help the division in which she works relocate. For personal reasons, she will not be relocating with the firm and will have to find another job at the end of the transition. What rewards could you offer? Here are some suggestions:

- Perhaps—when the work load starts to decrease—she would enjoy a couple of Friday afternoons off to give her family a head start on the weekend.

- Maybe there's a special skill that she could learn by attending a course, such as generating computer graphics.

- While doing tasks preparing for the transition, she may acquire special skills or experience that will enhance her résumé.

- She may be able to travel to the relocation site, meeting new people, seeing new places, and perhaps taking a weekend to see the local sights.

- In recognition of the completed project, you might take her *and* her spouse or significant other to dinner—sharing the celebration and enhancing her status.

- Based upon her extraordinary efforts, you might recommend that she receive a special bonus.

- You might give her your personal recommendation as a manager when she begins her job search and a commendation for her personnel file.

Depending upon your own circumstances you might be able to add other rewards or vary those listed. You would, of course, attend to her very natural need for security during this time of high change. Make sure she is aware of all severance benefits and explain changes in company plans as they affect her as soon as possible.

What About Everyday Humdrum Motivation?

But, you might say, a corporate relocation is an exceptional circumstance with special rules. What motivates staff in the daily routine—day after day, year after year? What motivates your staff to give that little bit extra during the summer doldrums and the winter blues?

Although you may not be able to use all of the techniques listed above, many of them are useful in all types of situations. Some may cost more than your budget can stand or set precedents which you cannot follow for all of your staff. Everyone has constraints: your budget may not allow you to take your staff and spouses to dinner or to give bonuses. Before you even begin to think of spending money, be sure to lay the groundwork properly:

- Pay your employees fairly in comparison to the pay scales of your organization, to their peers, and to the market. Follow the *same* rules for all salary actions.

- Be as fair as humanly possible. Try not to show favoritism. You will, most likely, enjoy the company of some members of your staff more than others. Be very careful not to show it. People sense preferences and rejection quickly, and their work performance will suffer from it. (You are less likely to make mistakes in major functions than in small details, unconsciously. Do you, for example, just happen to have lunch conferences more often with Mike because you enjoy his company?)

- Enrich the work of your employees whenever possible. Vary tasks and assignments. Boredom is your enemy; it can turn your employees into unproductive, sloppy automatons.

- If you have process workers, be sure to explain where the work comes from and what happens to it after their portion of the process. (It is astonishing that even some supervisors and middle managers don't know what happens to the products they and their employees produce. Many managers produce voluminous reports without the slightest idea how they are going to be used. This lack of understanding frequently leads to unfortunate speculation, poor-quality work, and resentment that spills over to other projects ("These reports are only used to fill up bookcases and make management feel important, so why should I bother to do them well?").

- Help employees to understand how their actions affect the overall performance of the organization. Be sure they are aware of their performance individually, as a department, and as a company. A clerk who has never been told about corporate performance can't be blamed for not caring about the fortunes of the company.

- Train and cross-train your staff. Most people like to learn. Additional skills make your employees more valuable to you and to themselves.

- Develop a winning team. Everyone likes to be a part of a success! Set high standards and share the rewards of winning. The atmosphere surrounding your staff members will encourage them to produce their best. If in moderation you recognize the accomplishments of the entire group and fail to provide that recognition when everyone does not contribute, peer pressure will help you in your task.

- Build the personnel files or portfolios of your staff. When appropriate take the time to provide permanent as well as temporary recognition. A pat on the back feels terrific but you can't put it on your résumé.

- Compliment up. If someone has done a terrific job, write to your boss complimenting the employee. It carries more punch than the same words directed to the employee.

- Don't hog the glory. If you are praised for work your staff completed, say so. It is part of your job to develop a staff that supports you well. (If you take full credit, someone will always find out—to your ultimate discredit.)

- PAY ATTENTION TO YOUR STAFF. EVERYONE WANTS TO BE SPECIAL. A SINCERE WORD OF THANKS CAN MAKE ALL THE DIFFERENCE.

Motivation Doesn't Have to Cost a Lot of Money

Rewards need not be expensive or time consuming. In fact, employees quite rightly dislike those who try to buy them. Honest praise, on the other hand, can do wonders. Try to make it a habit to write "well done" on at least one piece of work each day. If nothing comes across your desk that is excellent, pick the best of what you see. Employees will begin to look for your comments.

Try to develop special ways of letting your employees know that you are thinking of them. Some managers take their employees sailing or to Broadway plays; one distributes M&Ms. (*All* of the staff members from clerks to assistant vice presidents come by that manager's office to ask for M&Ms when they've worked particularly hard. The symbol is, of course, far more important than the small pieces of candy.)

Employees (Most of Them, Anyway) Are People

At the first of each year, list all of your employees' birthdays on your work calendar. Gifts are not necessary—a card or handwritten note will help make the person feel special. Remark on new clothes or hairstyles. Admire pictures of vacations, children, grandchildren, and vacations. Send an employee home two hours early (without mentioning it beforehand) on his or her anniversary and he or she will remember it for years. If you are not good at this type of personal detail, enlist the help of your secretary or chief of staff.

Notice the negative as well as the positive. Grief or worry may be lessened when shared, but don't pry. Employees are entitled to privacy should they want it. Remember, too, that it is *not* your role to be a psychiatrist, drug counselor, or personal financial consultant. Refer your employees with serious problems to appropriately qualified professionals.

Confidence: A Special Magic

It is a wonderfully warm feeling to know that someone believes and relies on you. One very important way to motivate people is to have faith in them. If someone whom you respect is depending upon the results of your efforts, you will work very hard not to let that person and yourself down. Many middle managers will walk across hot coals barefoot for a supervisor who believes in them. It is difficult to have faith and even more difficult to show it, but, if you can manage it, the results will astound you. If you don't really have confidence, don't fake it. The words "I'm counting on you to carry out this crucial task," while not as effective as "I know you will do this with your usual excellence" are still powerful. The employee will probably not be aware of the difference and will be able to detect your sincerity. And when you can, do have faith.

What's Sauce for the Goose Isn't Always Sauce for the Gander

Every employee is an individual. Never make the mistake of thinking they are all the same; you'll get burned (justifiably). You can't motivate everyone with the same techniques, you have to adjust them to each individual. Nonetheless, there are some useful generalizations to be made about different *categories* of staff members—people in similar jobs can usually be motivated in similar ways. Some short notes follow.

REPETITIVE WORKERS
When was the last time you spent eight solid hours photocopying? Try it sometime. You'll probably decide you've learned all you need to know after several hours. Stick it out and then multiply your feelings by the 220 working days in a year. Repetitive workers need recognition and to be made to feel that what they do is important. They need some variety whenever you can arrange it. They also need very clear standard͏͏ dging themselves against those standards, and ͏e longest) feedback when they are deviating If you don't care, why should they?

r employees who work on commission work for or a lot of gratuitous analysis and paperwork d to pay for it. Why should Fredrica spend an ts for nothing when that same hour could be missions? Since the skills are not the same, be p of promoting the best sales rep to the position both selling *and* managerial skills.

RESENTATIVES
ıblic—however much you like people—is wear-t burned out. (Burn-out means you've had it up you would normally handle easily will turn you

into a raving maniac.) Rotate jobs and provide a lot of reinforcement. This is one area where the manner in which you treat your employees will be directly reflected in the way they treat customers. After Herbert's paycheck has been late for the third time, he's likely to agree with a disgruntled customer that the service is lousy and help create a class-action suit.

PROFESSIONAL SPECIALISTS

These are the folks who frequently have management titles but don't actually manage people, and often don't particularly *want* to manage people: compensation experts, financial analysts, auditors, systems analysts . . . in short, all the techies. The techies often have much more loyalty to their profession than to your organization. Don't expect that they will be motivated by the same things that turn other managers on. Be very careful to help them maintain their knowledge base and their professional standing.

SECRETARIES

A great secretary is worth killing for. Make your secretary a part of your management team. Secretaries can run your office for you if you treat them as intelligent partners. It has lately become unfashionable to want to be a secretary. Too many secretaries are treated as nonpeople or as slaves instead of as people with important knowledge and skills. However, as a responsible manager, exercise caution before you promote your secretary. Make certain he or she has the skills and temperment for the position you are considering.

There's a reason for the caution. Many secretaries, even though they may not be in entry-level positions, share with entry-level employees one characteristic: much of their work is directed from above. Managers, on the other hand, must make judgemental decisions on a daily basis, they can't wait to be told what to do. Additionally, the quantifiers of success are very different for secretaries and managers. Without the familiar guideposts of a job well done, many secretaries find it difficult to know if they *are* doing a good job. The transition from one type of position to the other can be very difficult.*

---

*Before the massed secretaries of the world rise up in wrath to smite the authors, let us state that we have promoted several secretaries to managerial ranks. A majority of them had great difficulty with the transition. In the long run, the success rate in the new position was probably about the same for secretaries as it was for others, but the transition was generally much harder.

·opriate (there is *never* an excuse for prevent-
ising to his or her potential; good staff is hard
just take a long, hard look to make sure you
.

eople who learn very quickly, are aggressive,
ugh organizations quickly. Work with these
ergy to your mutual advantage. Just don't be
ou aren't doing anyone any favors by promot-
lore havoc has been wreaked by very intelli-
sons who lack skill in dealing with people and
anagers than by any number of slower plod-

ole game. It is enormously challenging and can
re innumerable factors to be applied in each
,o think about the background and age of your
oyees, for example, tend to be more concerned
employees are still trying to decide where and
the information you can gather, think, and use
member to like your employees when you can;
people among whom you will spend a large part

think that every employee is going to respond
rking 15 hours a day, six days a week. Some
be among your most expert workers—will want
work and go home. Unless the person is not
orily, you shouldn't take disciplinary action
r simply because he or she won't do *extra* work.
st cases no amount of motivation will alter their
ason lies in their personal motivation: they are
outside of work, which may be equally—or
hem.
need them too. While you might wish that
partment was totally work-oriented, remember
outside the office, and many of the people who
work and no more are giving that extra outside.
the mainstays of society. They run scout troops,
and help to create a place worth living in. It is
.

The Final Key to Employee Motivation

The last working day in June has ended and most of the employees of Mangled Manufacturing, Inc., have wended their way home, looking forward to the Fourth of July weekend, when they can perform the yearly rituals of burning hamburgers and blowing up family and friends with illegal firecrackers. Night is falling, and crickets and fireflies are singing and dancing in the fading light. Yet all is not well at MM's headquarters. The cleaning and security staffs are not alone. Huddled in their offices, executives at every level are hunched over their desks performing a different kind of yearly ritual. It is the time of year everyone in management dreads. On July 1, annual performance appraisals are due.

In the east wing of the sprawling headquarters, Lester Limpet stares down at the nearly completed appraisal of Terrence Truculent. Truculent is a fast-tracking supervisor transferred to Lester's department some nine months before. Lester reads Truculent's personnel file for the fifth time. He has received a steady stream of "Excellent—recommended for promotion" ratings. Previous managers have used "Remarks" section of the appraisal to rave about Truculent's work. Lester taps his teeth with a pencil. In the nine months he has supervised Truculent, Lester has seen little to support these glowing recommendations. Truculent has not really done well. He has shown flashes of brillance, but, in general, his performance has been uneven. Work has been left undone, and the quality of what has been done has been unreliable. Lester sighs. If he marks Truculent as anything less than excellent, he will probably have to explain why his opinion is so at variance with everyone elses'. He will be, in effect, disagreeing with all the other supervisors—Lester's peers—who have liked Truculent. A negative review will also end Truculent's fast-tracking, possibly permanently. Lester licks his lips, hesitates, then checks "Excellent—recommended for promotion."

Down the hall, Monty Minion completes the performance appaisal of Tracy Trueheart. For nine months Trueheart has turned in the best performance of any of Monty's staff. While not brillant, Trueheart was steady and dependable, always turning in competent work on time. Others in Monty's department sometimes outperformed Trueheart, but no one was so consistent and trustworthy. As a result, Monty allowed his supervision of her work to slip, trusting it would always get done. He continued to ignore her even when she was moved to a new position. Too late, Monty discovered Trueheart had an imperfect

working days since his last appraisal, you will have an impressive figure. For an insurance claims representative you might add up the approximate dollar saves or for a school bus driver the number of children-miles safely driven (35 children per day × an average of 20 miles per child × 170 days = 119,000 child-miles). Think about your staff. What can you recognize?

You probably will remember to include all the important criticisms in your appraisals, but be especially careful to include those accomplishments that the employee values. An easy way to do this, which also helps the employee prepare (at least mentally) for the review, is, about three weeks before the evaluation is due, remind the employee that his or her review is approaching and ask the employee to give you a handwritten list of his or her accomplishments during the appraisal period. You can include those you agree with and note for discussion any with which you don't agree.

But, Boss, You Said I Was Doing Good Work! Why Did You Rate Me At Standard?

Performance appraisals can backfire as a motivating tool if you are perceived as being unfair or inconsistent. Close your eyes and think about the worst (unfair, that is, not accurate but unflattering) appraisal you've received personally. It didn't make you want to work harder, did it? If you've never received an unfair or inadequate appraisal, count yourself lucky indeed and try to imagine what it might be like to be judged against standards you didn't know about or to be downgraded not because of your performance but because you didn't have a college degree. Even aside from biases, words mean different things to different people. Remember in the fifth grade when you had Miss Bates who was the "meanest" teacher in the whole school and your best friend—who had a different teacher—got better grades than you did even though you did better work? To the terrible Miss Bates, satisfactory meant a five-page report with no mistakes; to your friend's teacher, satisfactory meant a two-page report with less than five mistakes. You were experiencing the problems your employees face today. People are different, therefore, evaluations given by different people are different, even if theoretically, they are reviewing the same thing.

Is the solution to become an easy mark, give your employees the benefit of the doubt, and rate high? While some managers select this

option (and it surely is more pleasant to administer a positive evaluation than a mixed or negative one!), it does not help you or your
employees. Repeat: unless you have perfect employees working for
you, you do *not* help your employees by rating them undeservedly high
or by neglecting to document areas where they might improve. Your
staff won't find it easy to grow unless you help them. Of course, it is to
be hoped you will have employees who perform at or above standard,
and for clerical staff it may be sufficient to document the achievement
of those standards. (You'll want to add some recognition. More about
that in a minute.) But for supervisors, managers, and those who wish
to be promoted, you help them only by reinforcing what they do right
and pointing out where they can improve. In some cases, you may wish
to use some variation of the following wording: "As noted above, Jose
performs all of his current assignments at or above standard. However, Mr. Perez is interested in becoming a manager. To do so, he will
need to improve his writing skills. . . ."

If being an easy mark isn't the answer, what is? In order to write a
fair and useful performance appraisal, you need to:

- Base your evaluation on goals (standards) that were set *and* discussed at the beginning of the evaluation period.

- Formally and informally observe the employee *throughout* the
evaluation period and keep notes. (*Don't* trust your memory.)

- Discuss your observations with your employee frequently. (The
formal appraisal should never be a surprise to you or to your
employee. Watch your employee's face carefully while he or she is
reading your written comments. In most cases, you will be able to
see what he or she is feeling. If he or she seems surprised, it means
you are not communicating well enough.)

- In so far as is possible, use objective data. (For example, either
someone met budget or he didn't; either timeliness standards were
met 98 percent of the time or they weren't.) For your managers and
supervisors, however, you will need to evaluate some skills less
amenable to direct measurement, such as political skills. In those
cases, be sure to use specific examples and the *results* of these
actions and try to be as fair as you can.

- Apply your judgment uniformly. (What is rated below standard
performance for Dot must also be evaluated as below standard for

Alexei.) There is a tendency to have a creeping lowering of standards as managers try to reward the hard work of their employees. Hard work should be rewarded, but it is not the same thing as performance above standard. There are other ways to reward employees than money and promotions. Base your promotions on demonstrated ability, skill and aptitude, and hard work. Far too many companies are littered with the skeletons of managers who were promoted as a reward. There are other ways to reward people.

- Tell both sides of the story; be sure to include both strengths and weaknesses. (It is as important to tell Henrietta what she is doing right as it is to record what needs improvement. Reinforce desired behavior so that it will be repeated.) And be careful not to blow a single incident out of proportion; keep a sense of perspective.

- Really spend the time and effort to write the best appraisal you can. Perhaps you will want to write your evaluations when you are completely relaxed and at home with complete quiet and a glass of wine.

Performance Appraisals for Fun and Profit—Part II: Fun

Performance reviews *can* be fun, especially with good performers. You can review goal achievement, review improvement needs, and then discuss something employees always want to discuss—career development. You and your employee can share a sense of accomplishment and teamwork.

On the other hand, bad news rarely promotes a good time. Although there is no way to make a bad appraisal enjoyable, you can be prepared for it and minimize the suffering.

Whether you have good or bad news, be sure to set aside a completely private and uninterrupted hour to go over the review you have written. The review may be stressful for both of you—so be as relaxed as you can be at the beginning. Unless the appraisal is excellent, don't do it over lunch or dinner. Indigestion doesn't help (although you may want to schedule the interview for late in the day and take the employee for a drink). Even if the appraisal contains some significant problems, remember to recognize the human being you are evaluating. Unless you plan to fire the person shortly, don't destroy your relationship.

In order to make the appraisal truly useful, give your employee time to digest what you've written and then discuss it. Since some employees will be unable to think "on the spot," you should always allow your employee at least 24 hours to ponder your comments. At the end of this time you may need to schedule a second meeting, which might be longer but will probably be more productive than the first. Many companies require the employee's signature on the appraisal form and give the employee room to comment. This is an excellent practice and it insures that no appraisal—particularly a negative one—is filed without the employee's knowledge.

Accuracy Is More Important Than Your Pride

If an employee asks you to change something you have written in a review, try not to be threatened. You remain in control. Consider carefully the reasons for the requested change; don't be intimidated or forced, but be fair. If the employee is right, change it. Remember, one of your purposes is motivation, and an employee who is wronged will do far more damage to the morale of a department than changing what you've written will do to your authority as a manager.

This Still Sounds Like a Lot of Work. What's in It for Me?

If you have good people, spending the time to motivate them will help you create a great staff that not only helps you to accomplish your goals and represents you well when you are unavailable (sick or on vacation) but also makes your daily working life a pleasure. In short, a staff that delivers peak performance. Aside from the other benefits, it's more fun to spend the better part of your waking hours with people who know what they are doing than it is to spend your days making corrections and apologies and repeating instructions for the hundredth time. Managers with a track record of good staff motivation are among the first to be promoted.

If you don't yet have a terrific staff, getting them motivated will help you to make the best of the situation and to get the best performance possible. And if you've used performance appraisals properly, you'll already have your reasons (and your efforts to correct the situation) in writing if you have to change your staffing. That can be important in how *you* are judged by your superiors (and in case of employee law suits).

Can You Be Too Successful?

If you motivate your staff in this manner, it will soon become obvious that your people really produce. It won't take long before that is recognized by others within your organization—who may become headhunters. While you shouldn't give up so many of your staff at one time that your performance begins to suffer, never stand in the way of a good opportunity for one of your employees. You are only cutting your own throat.

The employee *will* learn of the missed opportunity despite any assurances to the contrary you are given. Naturally, he or she will be resentful and you will lose the support you were trying to retain. If you honestly think the proposed job isn't right for your staff member, explain why and then allow the employee to make his or her own decision.

Motivating employees is always a tricky business for the simple reason that every person is different. Although what works for one person will not necessarily work for another, there are certain basics which, applied with intelligence, will get results. Above all, think: how do *you* want to be treated by *your* superiors?

Motivation may seem like a lot of work but it's worth the effort. Recognition and frequent performance reviews (both formal and informal) help keep your employees working towards the targets *you* set. A properly motivated staff will produce far more work—and the quality will be better as well. In the long run, you'll look better and work *less* hard because your staff is working harder. You might even be able to relax and plan your next career move.

11

Who Do You Want to Be? Choosing a Leadership Style

Just as you should establish a working relationship with every manager you work for, you should select a style of leadership appropriate to the group you are leading. A short case history will demonstrate the reason for this.

Richard

Richard was an excellent middle manager, working his way up rapidly at Western Buggywhip & Misericord. He had developed a very informal style that allowed the supervisors who worked for him considerable freedom. He worked very hard and met—in fact, exceeded—his objectives.

His management style was very easygoing. Although he kept close tabs on his staff, his supervision was unobtrusive. He had confidence in them and let them have considerable freedom. The overall impression he fostered was "try anything you want—if it works, great; if not, we'll try something else."

His staff responded well to his trust. They liked him and worked very hard not only to meet divisional objectives but also to see who could be the most creative or inventive. As a result of his department's

143

success, Richard was offered a promotion and a chance to work in a different division.

Richard quickly established a good relationship with his boss and his peers. However, after three months, two of the three managers reporting to him requested transfers and the remaining manager was clearly unhappy. The personnel department spoke with Richard's boss, citing the complaints voiced by the managers who had requested transfers: Richard didn't understand the division's objectives; he failed to give his subordinates any direction; he didn't care what was happening; he expected too much of his staff; he provided no leadership at all. All three subordinate managers thought Richard was a disaster as a manager.

When his boss reviewed this information with Richard, he was devastated. His greatest strength had always been his ability to manage people. He had recognized there were some problems in his new department, but felt they were adjustment problems and would pass with time. He had no inkling that his people were so unhappy or that his performance was in question.

"You're right, Mr. Grimley, that was a terrible idea!"

What was Richard's problem? He had tried to run his new department as he had run his old one, without considering whether the style that had succeeded previously was appropriate to the new job. He had expected people who didn't know him to work on the same basis of trust and minimal direction as people who had worked with him for a long time. Simply put, he had failed to adapt his leadership style to the situation.

A number of factors help to determine what style of leadership best suits the leader, his or her followers, and the situation. In the middle of a fire, you don't call a meeting to decide how best to deal with the situation. The leader tells people what to do. On the other hand, a new manager, fresh from graduate school, won't be very successful telling an accountant with 30 years' experience how to prepare the corporate tax forms he has submitted on behalf of the company for the past ten years. Based on the manager's relative lack of experience and the accountant's clear competence, at most the manager can consult, drawing on the employee's experience and building up the mutual trust necessary to the manager-employee relationship. Effective leadership depends on the elements of the situation. What will work well in one case will be completely wrong in another.

Styles of Leadership

One of the frequently used models of leadership (developed by Tannenbaum and Schmidt) is based on the amount of authority used solely by the leader contrasted with the decision-making authority shared with the group. There are four commonly-recognized styles (which may have slightly different labels in other material you may read). One manager may use all four styles during the course of a day. (Jonas Jakowski of the Coal Tar Candy Company will provide an example for each style.) The styles are:

TELLING

In this style, managers *tell* their employees what to do. They make all decisions without consulting their employees, observe employee performance, and reward or punish behavior accordingly.

As Jonas walks up to the print shop, he is thinking about the previous print shop manager, who was very directive. The report he is bringing to be printed is a key part of the materials for the upcoming directors' meeting. Time is short and the materials must be perfect.

He assembles the print shop workers and begins to explain about the upcoming meeting. He is interrupted by Tom, who is the lead printer and is also the union shop steward, who says "just tell us what to do, man." The others seem to agree. Although not his favorite style, Jonas complies and tells them what to do.

SELLING

This style is often confused with telling. Managers make operational decisions without consulting the employees involved. After decisions are made, however, the manager presents the decisions to the employees with explanations. He or she thus tries to convince—*sell*—the work force into believing or understanding that the decisions are the best choice for the situation.

Leaving the print shop, Jonas reviews the new Black as Tar candy campaign which his young sales force must begin to implement in two weeks. He doesn't really like it and believes his staff will not like it either. It is important, since they must implement it, that his staff believe in the campaign. The campaign was developed by Jonas's boss and is not subject to change. He reviews the *selling* strategy that he will be using to present the campaign to his staff. He then holds a meeting of the sales staff to present the campaign using the sales techniques explained in Chapter 3.

CONSULTING

Managers using this style ask employees for their opinions on how best to approach certain decisions. By following this *consulting* process, the managers are sharing some of their authority—the right to decide. Decisions are then presented with explanations and reference to the suggestions from the group. Managers who consult use less force (direct use of authority, such as firings, changes in salary and rank and, other disciplinary measures), but always retain the right to use force when necessary.

Having sold his sales staff on the Black as Tar campaign, Jonas hurries to a staff meeting with his senior managers. He is looking forward to the meeting because his senior managers are a committed, experienced group. They share an easy camaraderie. Among other things on the agenda, Jonas has a problem which he wants to consult with them about. He has a clear idea of the result he wants to achieve, but has not been able to develop a specific method of implementation. He wants to listen to his mangers' ideas before he makes up his mind.

JOINING

In this style, managers define the objectives, then *join* the work group in reaching them. When joining their employees, managers delegate all of their authority and disciplinary power except in extreme situations. Decisions are made by the group or by individuals within the group.

CHART 11.1

MANAGEMENT STYLES

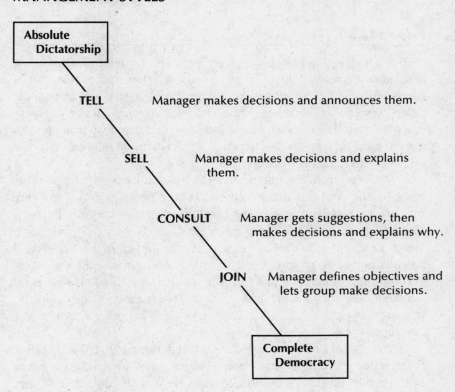

Experience has shown that it is easier to move up the scale (use more authority) than it is to move down. Employees tend not to trust authoritarian managers (the TELL style) who suddenly decide to join the group.

Jonas is still wiping tears of laughter from his eyes (a result of the parody Coal Tar Miner who has represented the company in recent TV ads), when he is reminded by his secretary that it is time to leave for lunch. It is a working lunch with his peers intended to develop a nuclear-emergency evacuation plan. He wonders for the hundredth time why he was selected for this project. He has neither experience nor knowledge in disaster planning. Neither, it seems, do any of his peers. Perhaps by sharing the knowledge and skills they have they will be able to construct something valuable. Jonas hopes so. He has very little authority to force his peers to participate effectively. By joining them, he plans to move the project as quickly as he can.

Responsibility

Before examining the elements comprising a leadership situation, a note about responsibility. In all cases, of course, the manager is responsible for the results. A manager may delegate authority, but, unless given specific instructions from above, may never delegate responsibility. It may seem harsh, but it is a fact of managerial life: you are responsible for the satisfaction of departmental goals and the actions of your subordinates.

An incident from the columns of the newspapers can help to illustrate this concept. As it was reported in the press, a group of Army recruits—a platoon—was being marched past the tent of the commanding general of an Army training base. They were chanting a "song" as an aid to unified movement. At the end of the chant, several recruits added an unauthorized rider one newspaper called a "barnyard epithet." The general heard the addition and the battalion commanding officer, a major, was brought up on charges for failing to properly discipline his men. The major was transferred to a less prestigious post.

To put this in perspective, you must understand that the battalion commander was at least three management levels above the person in actual command (the "subordinate manager") of the detachment that made the remark—and *was not present* at the time it happened. Nevertheless, he was held responsible.

Of course, this is an extreme case. In the army, the commanding officer is responsible for *everything* that occurs in his command. It is unlikely that, in a corporate environment, a manager would be disciplined because an employee shouted an obscenity outside the president's office (although you *might* be disciplined if, say, an office party held in your department got out of hand). Nonetheless, it illustrates the principle of responsibility. Recruits are expected to be disciplined. The offense was a breach of discipline—meaning that the manager with ultimate responsibility for the discipline of his department, in this case the commander of the training battalion—had failed to institute adequate procedures or to oversee his subordinates properly. He was held to have failed to meet his organizational objectives and was transferred laterally. The same thing can occur in a corporate situation. You can not delegate responsibility.

Key Elements in Determining a Management Style

Based upon the situation, a manager chooses a style either retaining or sharing authority for the way in which objectives are to be achieved. As a manager, how do you decide—what are the criteria—for adopting a particular style?

There are eight areas to consider:

AREA ONE

You should consider the amount of authority or force you have. Can you—without referring to anyone else—hire, fire, and promote those who work for you? If so you have complete authority and can, at least as far as this factor is concerned, choose any style. If you have some authority but it is less than complete (as is the case with most managers), you should select a style somewhere in the sell-consult range. If you have no real authority, you must join, as you have no way of compelling others to abide by your decisions.

AREA TWO

Analyze the leadership styles previously experienced by the group. Groups tend to respond best to those styles with which they are familiar. If the group is accustomed to being directed and checked in their daily work, don't join them as they will be confused and suspicious. If you consult with them, they are likely to think you are asking *them* to do *your* job. Generally speaking, a group that has been "told" will feel most comfortable in a tell situation. (If *you* are comfortable only in a join or consult style, you may be able to introduce it gradually, but to introduce it all at once will not work—as Richard found out.) If your employees have a mixed set of experiences or have never worked together, choose the compromise styles, sell or consult. They have the greatest chance of unifying a diverse group into a productive and creative whole.

Although it may seem like a cliche, there are some work habits that can be attributed to nations. For example, Americans and Swedes tend to expect to be consulted, while Germans and Greeks have a stronger cultural expectation of being directed in the work place. Should you be employed by a multinational corporation, study the history and business culture of a group before you decide upon a style. (The business magazines of a country will often provide a clue, as will management books published in the country or about the country.) Add this component—based on study not cliche—to your analysis.

AREA THREE

Remember that the old adage "when in Rome, do as the Romans do" applies to more than table manners. Consider the styles used by your manager and your manager's manager. If you are operating in a consult environment, your manager will expect you to consider the suggestions made by your employees and may consult with them in person from time to time. Your employees will see their peers in other departments participating in the decision-making process and will feel left out if you don't ask for their help. Similarly, if your manager is authoritarian, he or she will not only direct you, but also your subordinates and your interactions with them.

AREA FOUR

Analyze the attitude of your employees toward you, each other, and the work to be accomplished. On a sliding scale, begin by joining or consulting with a group that is committed, eager, and mature. Move up the scale to a more sell-oriented style as you work with groups whose attitude is less positive. A tell style is clearly appropriate when you are managing hostile or immature staff members.

AREA FIVE

The amount of time you have to make a decision, and the amount of time you and your staff have to complete your area's objectives also plays a role in determining the appropriate leadership style. If you have a long time in which to make a decision, your style can be any of the four. If you must make a decision quickly, obviously you must do it by yourself or consult only a few selected staff members. Remember that the camel is reputed to be a horse designed by a committee that had seven years to complete the design. On the other hand, once the decision has been made, if the time allotted to perform the task is short, your efforts (by joining the group) will help get the job done. Here, too, if the time is sufficient, any leadership style as determined by other factors will be appropriate.

AREA SIX

Consider the relative expertise and experience both you and the group have:

CONDITION	STYLE INDICATOR
Your employees have less experience than you do.	tell
Your employees have more experience than you do.	consult
Both of you are experienced.	any style
Neither is experienced.	join

AREA SEVEN

There are, in addition, several miscellaneous factors which will have a strong influence on your decision when they are present:

CONDITION	STYLE INDICATOR
The job is highly repetitive and boring.	tell
The key information is confidential.	tell
The job is strenuous or dangerous.	join

(In regard to the last, take the example of the Army again. A good leader says "Follow me!" not "Attack over there!")

AREA EIGHT

Finally—and this is very important—you must consider the styles with which you are most comfortable. A manager who really doesn't believe in joining will appear forced and unnatural in group decision making and, consequently, less effective. The group will quickly realize the manager really doesn't want to join and will participate less than is needed to make the technique successful. The same is true at the other end of the scale. If you simply can't tell people what to do without consulting, forcing yourself into a tell mode will be just as unsuccessful.

It should be obvious by now that the more flexible you are, the larger the number of situations you can manage appropriately. The manager who can shift from tell to consult, who can join when necessary and sell when needed, will do well regardless of the type of staff he or she must manage. The lesson is clear: if you want to be promoted, develop your ability to manage different situations in different ways and learn to recognize when each type of management is required.

In the case study at the beginning of this chapter, Richard had gotten himself into trouble by using the wrong management style. There is a shortcut that would have indicated to him what style he should have used.

Chart 11.2 has been filled with Richard's responses. By tabulating his answers, giving a full point to an unequivocal answer and fractions when more than one answer applies, a weighted score is determined.

Although Richard's preferred mode is consult, the chart indicates he should either tell or sell. However, since he had points in both the consult and join columns, the balance should be tipped towards sell. If you think about the complaints his subordinate managers made about him, you can see that this would be the right mode. They wanted more direction, more leadership—which tilts the scale towards tell—but Richard was used to a consult-join environment. A sell style will give his managers the direction they are used to while setting the groundwork for the kind of interaction—consulting—that Richard likes.

As with all tools, don't slavishly follow this model. You must temper the results you get with common sense and your own experience. Nonetheless, these techniques will give you a leg up on adapting your methods to the needs of your environment.

Chart 11.3 has been left blank. Fill it in for yourself, then study your results. Compare the style indicated to the style you now use. If you are already doing what you should be, fine. If the chart shows you should be using a different method, consider it carefully. Are there problems in your department that might be eliminated if your style

CHART 11.2

DETERMINING A MANAGEMENT STYLE
KEY ELEMENTS

ELEMENT	YOUR SITUATION	MANAGEMENT STYLE			
		TELL	SELL	CONSULT	JOIN
1. Your authority	- I recommend hiring, firing, salary, etc. - My decisions are approved by 2 layers of management.		X		
2. Employees' previous leadership experience	My employees have experienced several different leadership styles.		X		
3. Management style environment	Senior management is generally tell — with some selling.	X			
4. Employees' attitude	My employees are mature and skilled but skeptical about management — and me in particular.		X		
5. Time allotted • for decision	Very tight deadline.	X			
• for task	Sufficient	Any	style.		
6. Relative experience	- I have education in this area and other management experience. My employees have lots of experience in this area.			X	
7. Miscellaneous factors	The key information is confidential.	X			
8. Your preferred style	I am laid-back. I like to join in with my employees on projects.				X
SUBTOTALS		3	③	1	1

CHART 11.3

DETERMINING A MANAGEMENT STYLE
KEY ELEMENTS

ELEMENT	YOUR SITUATION	MANAGEMENT STYLE			
		TELL	SELL	CONSULT	JOIN
1. Your authority					
2. Employees' previous leadership experience					
3. Management style environment					
4. Employees' attitude					
5. Time allotted • for decision					
• for task					
6. Relative experience					
7. Miscellaneous factors					
8. Your preferred style					
SUBTOTALS					

was different? Would things run more smoothly? Would you be more comfortable in the style indicated than in the one you are using? (Many managers feel they must be authoritative without realizing that other styles can work as well or better.) You may be surprised.

Good Grief! Do I Have to Go Through All This Each Time I Need to Make a Decision?

Of course not. This book is intended to make life as a manager easier, not harder.

You should go through this process if you enter into a new job or your current situation changes, for instance, if you get a new boss. The first few times you go through this process it *will* seem complicated and laborious, although the results will make the labor worthwhile. After you have used these methods a few times, you will find it unnecessary to go through the whole process. Much of this will have become second nature to you, and you will find yourself instinctively performing this kind of analysis without going through the formal process.

You may decide to project a different style in staff meetings than you do with your subordinates. If you have managers working directly under you, you might, for example, find it works best to consult or join with those subordinate managers while you tell or sell to the rest of your staff. Frequently, as your relationship with your boss and with your subordinates improves over time, you can change your style, sliding from tell to sell to consult to join. Among the most crucial lessons a manager can learn is that no situation stays the same forever. Staff members are promoted or fired or retire; new faces arrive to replace those who have left or to take up new positions created to meet changing corporate objectives. The techniques discussed in this chapter will stand you in good stead whatever the change.

Above all be aware of the different styles of management and find the modes with which *you* are most comfortable. It will do you little good to decide on a tell mode of managing if you are so uncomfortable that you do it badly. As with establishing a relationship, the essence is compromise. You must find the style that is best for you *and* the situation. You may have to adopt a style other than the one analysis indicates is optimal if that optimal style is impossible for you. However, an awareness of the clash between the style dictated by the situation and one you are capable of will help defuse problems before they become serious; you will be expecting them.

12

Delegation: Why You Do It, When to Do It, How to Do It

Delegation: after "bottom line" this is the management buzz word heard most often. Everyone believes in delegation; it's like home, motherhood, and apple pie. It's also one of those concepts that is honored most often with lip-service rather than action. The odds are that, at any one time, most managers are failing to delegate properly.

Of course, if *you* aren't currently delegating, there's a *very* good reason why it's impossible, right? No doubt you agree, though, that it's the correct thing for everyone else! Of course you would.

Why is this technique so loudly acknowledged but so frequently found not to apply to *this* special situation or *that* unusual task? What can you do to avoid falling into this trap?

Why Delegate?

Because it's your job. First and foremost as a manager or supervisor (or as someone who hopes to join the ranks of management), your job is to get things done through other people . . . in other words, to delegate. Unless you are a staff specialist with no employees reporting to you, you can't get the job done by yourself. You are paid to manage, not perform every task. Every successful manager is expected to do some tasks—as opposed to managing the completion of those tasks—occasionally. The danger lies in the definition of occasionally. It is clear to Edwardo Superb, director of customer service for International

Interchangeables, Inc., that he physically can't answer all 60 telephone lines that come into his center. It is less clear to him that his subordinate managers are capable of learning to handle the preparation for the budget and monthly financial cycle. So he does it all himself, burning the midnight oil, complaining all the while. He'd rather go home early. What's stopping him?

He hasn't learned to delegate.

Okay, Why Don't Managers Delegate?

The primary reason managers don't delegate is that they become perfectionists. And of course the only person who can perform to a perfectionist's standards is him- or herself. The chief executive officer of a major, nation-wide corporation confessed recently that he didn't really like the letters his senior vice presidents presented for his signature. He knew he could do better and had to restrain himself on a daily basis from redoing the work. Even if he could write better letters, his job was to cement large sales and to chart the future of the company—not to write ten letters a day. Yet he had to fight against the urge *not* to delegate.

Persons who succeed do so because (for the most part) they are good at what they do. Naturally, they want things done not just well, but the *best* they can be. However, learning to delegate means learning to accept some imperfections. Since people can't learn without making some mistakes, a successful manager's job is to see that the mistakes aren't too serious and to pick up his subordinate, brush her off, and start her working again. Learning to accept imperfections, however, doesn't mean foresaking standards entirely. Proper delegation, with the right coaching and follow up, will result in increasingly accurate, perhaps even "perfect" work.

Delegation also means accepting styles that are different from yours. Just because the solution your supervisor or manager implements is different from the solution you would have chosen doesn't mean it is inferior.

The second reason managers give for not delegating is closely related to the first. It is much harder, they say, to clean up the mess than to do it yourself in the first place. Besides (they whine), it takes time to delegate properly, and I don't have the time or the staff to do it right. Even if this is true (sometimes it is; frequently it isn't), if you don't delegate and suffer through the clean up, you're dooming yourself to burn the midnight oil forever. You'll never develop subordinates who can carry part of your work load, and *your* management will find you virtually unpromotable since you have not prepared a successor.

The third reason why managers don't delegate is fear: they're afraid that if their staff members know how to do all or part of their jobs they will become redundant, perhaps even be fired, and their staff members promoted in their places. Keep in mind, whether or not you delegate, you are the manager; you make the final decisions. It is particularly true at this moment that with the postwar baby-boom-population bulge, there are more qualified managers with high expectations than there are senior positions for those people. Not delegating is no protection against competition; you will always have it. If you delegate well, however, you'll have a step up on the competition because you'll have more time to devote to your job, managing; and your area will produce more work, because you won't be the only one doing it!

The fourth reason some managers give for not delegating is that they don't think of it. You don't have that excuse any more.

Some Extra Bennies of Delegation

Aside from it being an important part of your job you will also reap some perhaps unexpected benefits from delegating well. First, it is a part of investing in your staff. When a staff member has worked particularly hard on a project, you can provide a reward in the opportunity to learn something new. Secondly, effective delegation will help you to create a succession plan—bringing up managers who can replace you when it is time for you to move on. Thirdly, delegation can free some of your time to learn new skills and prepare yourself for new opportunities. All in all, how can you miss?

What Should You Delegate?

You should, depending upon the circumstances, be able to delegate almost everything that you do. The key to success is to break the job into measurable units, and then, of course, to measure progress as it occurs. Begin by delegating small units of work, and increase the load gradually—culminating in entire projects—as both you and the employee become accustomed to the process. During the budget cycle, for example, you might begin by delegating one area or line—facilities, equipment, or associated travel expense. If you have no one capable of handling more than one area, choose several employees and have each one handle a different area. Next time, choose the employee who caught on fastest—suppose her name is Judith—and increase her responsibility by having her develop a first cut (assembling all the data prepared by employees handling individual areas or lines as she did last year). The third time around Judith can prepare the entire budget for your review and adjustments before final presentation.

Any project can be broken into smaller pieces—reducing some of your workload and helping your employees to gain experience without being overwhelmed. You can even divide managerial responsibility into learning units. Use the time you will be away and your degree of accessibility as the means of division. First leave Joseph in charge while you are at an all-day meeting (and can be easily reached by telephone); then while you are on a three-day trip; finally have him stand in while you go on vacation for two weeks (without a telephone).

If you should be able to delegate all of your responsibilities, why does your organization need you? To keep the whole together, to decide what to delegate, and to insure that those tasks delegated are completed correctly. Just because you are able to delegate a task does not mean that you *choose* to do so or that the task will be done as well as if you manage it carefully. Those managers who are most successful choose what they delegate very carefully and keep corporate politics in mind. Even though your chief of staff may know your budget inside and out, you should, for example, choose to make your budget presentation yourself. You have the ultimate responsibility; only you can make those critical decisions in the force of the moment.

There are three other reasons you might choose to do something your staff could do just as well: (1) you suspect there are political ramifications your staff may not be able to handle, (2) you need the visibility, and (3) you enjoy the task! Just keep in mind that almost everything can be delegated. When you find yourself thinking that you are unable to delegate, it is a danger sign.

When Should You Delegate?

From your first day on the job to your last. Use common (unfortunately, rather uncommon) sense, however. Don't delegate something until you understand it thoroughly and can control the process. It is also inappropriate to dump something on someone else just because you don't like to do it or don't understand it. (On the other hand, there is nothing wrong with having your chief of staff prepare presentations if you hate to do it and he loves it. Just be careful that, if you always assign certain tasks to others, you still know how to do them yourself. If you don't, you run the risk of a gap in your own managerial knowledge and education, and promotions come more often to the well-rounded manager than to the specialist.)

To Whom Do You Delegate?

Selecting the right employee for the job is an art as well as a skill. Chapter 9 has some useful techniques for hiring the right employee, and you can use some of those same techniques to select the right employee for each task. Consider all of your staff members when making decisions about delegation. Sometimes you will wish to select an employee who is most ready for the size and complexity of the task you have in mind. Other times you will want to choose someone, for development purposes, who has little experience in the area. Of course, be certain that the employee has the time and support needed to complete the job. Here, as always, be careful not to discriminate against certain staff members. If you do not continue to develop *all* of your staff, you will loose flexibility.

One further caveat: do not attempt to teach someone to keep confidential information quiet by delegating a task that involves private information. Use your knowledge of your staff here. Someone who has fed confidential information to the grapevine (or a competitor) will most likely do it again—even if he or she promises not to do so.

Delegation with Style

Like most other management tasks, good delegation is a matter of sound planning, clear communication, and belief in your employees. Follow these easy steps:

1. Select a task that you understand thoroughly and that can be broken into smaller projects which you can monitor easily.

2. Select an employee who has the background and skills to enable him or her to learn the new task.

3. Set up the task so that you can explain it clearly. Obtain all of the necessary reference materials and job aids. Think through appropriate due dates with frequent intermittent checks. (If you find the employee is doing well, you can reduce the number of checks at a later time.)

4. Thoroughly brief the employee on the task. Place it in perspective. Explain why you chose this person for this task. Discuss the approach the employee will take and review the due dates.

5. It is VERY IMPORTANT that at this point you express your confidence in the person you have chosen.

6. Make sure the employee has not only the responsibility but also the authority to get the job done. Advise all those who need to know of the new assignment. (If you assign responsibility without the requisite authority, you are setting your employee and yourself up for failure.)

7. Stay out of the way and let the employee do the job.

8. Faithfully follow up on all of the interim dates you set. (If you don't keep a tickler file, set one up.) Encourage, correct, help. Keep the project on track.

9. When the project has been completed, give the employee credit—publicly, if appropriate.

10. Review the entire project to make sure the employee can apply what he or she has learned.

11. Relax. You've earned it—and besides, since your employees are helping with the work, you have the time.

A Delegation Case Study

It is a Sunday afternoon in late summer when Sandy Silberger receives a phone call at home. Tommy Terrible, chief of staff to Randy Randazzo, president of Randy's Rodent Rentals, Inc., is on the line. Listening to the tension in Tommy's voice, Sandy resigns herself to whatever follows. After much fuss, Tommy says that he and his secretary, Susan Soulfull, have been working all weekend on the materials for Randy's presentation to the board. All of the photocopying machines in the building are broken and there is no point in continuing today. Still, all of the material must be ready by Thursday noon when Randy and Tommy fly to Chicago for the board meeting.

There are slides to be prepared and reproduced. Sandy has prepared many such booklets and, Tommy reminds her, he, Tommy, also has the responsibility for the new advertising campaign. Tommy pauses. Will she take over the budget booklets?

Knowing she must, Sandy agrees—sighing mentally as she reviews her already packed schedule for the upcoming week. Upon inquiring, she learns—as she has suspected—that the draft of the booklet is only about one-half complete.

STEP ONE

Because she has herself prepared as well as managed the preparation of many such projects, Sandy knows the process thoroughly. She will not have time to do it all herself but can delegate major portions of the project. Sandy breaks the preparation into three major tasks: (1) development of the numbers, text, and illustrations, (2) typesetting, paste-up, and proofing and verifying numbers, and (3) selecting and managing a printer.

STEP TWO

Because of the tight time pressure and the critical nature of the task, Sandy decides to select three people who have already demonstrated the technical expertise to handle their respective assignments. This will not be primarily a learning experience for her subordinates, although, her staff assistant, Ready, will gain some additional needed supervisory experience.

STEP THREE

Sandy arrives at work early on Monday to review the work already completed on the RRR budget book. She makes five copies of the materials and of the time tables for each of the three subsidiary projects. The schedule calls for frequent reviews, sometimes by telephone or by her senior manager when she is out of the office. In no case does a subordinate go longer than half a day between reviews. She makes a brief check of inventory, noting those items which may need to be purchased quickly. She also picks up samples of booklets her staff has produced in the past with similarities to the budget book.

STEP FOUR

At 9:30 A.M. Sandy holds a meeting with the three staff members she has selected—Freddy, Ready, and Teddi—and her chief of staff, Sam. She gives a brief background of the project, stressing the work already complete, the importance of the booklet, and the tight time frame. She relates this task to other highly successful booklets produced by this staff. She then reviews the assignments and passes out the time checks. After a thorough discussion and question period, Freddy, Ready, and Teddi seem to understand their assignments and are ready to get to work. Nonetheless, they express some concern over the deadline. Sandy reviews the tight-but-possible time frame and reminds everyone to be sure to raise problems as soon as they are discovered. As a part of her active leadership, she volunteers to obtain the missing data.

STEP FIVE

Sandy is careful to conclude the meeting by expressing her confidence in the staff and reminds them of the high visibility of the RRR book. She will insure that they receive the proper recognition for their efforts.

STEP SIX

As the meeting breaks up, Sam confirms with Sandy that he will make sure that Freddy, Ready, and Teddi's new assignment is well known—along with the time frame. He offers to run interference for them to be sure they have the supplies, equipment, and time to complete their part of the project.

STEP SEVEN

Both Sandy and Sam have other matters demanding their immediate attention. They have no problem letting their employees work on their own. Their concerns are minimized by the frequent checks built into the schedule.

STEP EIGHT

After her 10:30 meeting, Sandy meets Teddi in the hall and learns that two printers will submit verbal bids before noon, but that the third printer they use frequently is closed. Sandy gives her the name of another printing house to try. Sam holds a project review at noon and finds that things are moving along well. One of the word processors has gone home with the flu and Sam gives Ready the authority to pay for temporary help even though it will be very expensive. Sandy holds the afternoon review and shows her delight at the progress made. The group helps Freddy with the rewording of the conclusion. The right words have somehow been eluding him.

In this fashion, the project proceeds. Sandy mediates a strong disagreement between Freddy and Ready over layout. Sam helps Teddi to work with the purchasing department to secure a purchase order verbally. Review meetings are held regularly. Both Sandy and Sam make a special effort to be available to their staff members.

STEP NINE

Not without some mishaps, the books are completed just in time and sent via messenger to Tommy and Randy with a note from Sandy mentioning the efforts of her staff—Sam, Freddy, Ready, and Teddi. She copies her staff on the memo and adds a handwritten note of thanks on their copies. She is particularly pleased by a special phone call of thanks from Randy, who calls from Chicago just after having had the opportunity to study the finished product. She asks Ready to help spread the word.

STEP TEN

At the next regularly scheduled staff meeting, Sandy passes out copies of the RRR budget book and tells her staff that they played an important part in helping Randy's Rodent Rentals with the funding for next year. At her request, Freddy, Ready, and Teddi, talk about the production and share with the rest of the staff the new things they have learned. Sam summarizes by remarking that now that Randy and Tommy know how effective this department is, further requests are sure to follow. Everyone on the staff must become familiar with the process. He and Sandy answer additional questions.

STEP ELEVEN

That night Sandy and Sam relax over a drink on the way home. The type of thorough delegation and completed staff work they have just demonstrated will stand them both in good stead. After a while the talk turns from careers to football and family picnics.

Oops! Take Your Feet Off the Desk!

What happens when you've followed all of the steps to delegation faithfully and suddenly you have a mess? Irate managers are calling at the rate of two a minute. The schedule you promised last week was not published and a poorly written memo with several mistakes purported to take its place.

Although you might have been a little uneasy when you selected a specific employee for this task, you had no choice; there was no one else. Since resources are limited, all management includes compromise. How do you pick up the pieces?

As always, it depends on the specifics of the situation. Before you do anything else, speak directly with the employee involved. Although you may not agree with his or her version of the situation, you owe it to your staff to get the information directly—not secondhand with embellishments. Clear your mind and listen carefully. Think about solutions later; now you need data. Your handling of the employee will depend upon the situation as you see it, including past performance and mitigating circumstances. If discipline is in order, do it in private. Unless the employee is irretrievable, try to leave him or her on the project but increase the number and thoroughness of the reviews.

Then take some time to work through various remedies. Be sure to consider several alternatives before selecting one. What has happened is history. A little more time won't hurt the situation and may save you from getting egg on your face twice! When you are thinking about solutions, try to install permanent processes rather than temporary fixes. Set up policies and procedures that will prevent the problem from reoccurring. Then fix the problem with as little defensiveness as possible and, again, if possible, with the help of the employee who made the mistake in the first place. Do not point your finger at the erring staff member; it is also your responsibility. And studies show that employees work far less hard for managers who do not support them in times of trouble.

The problem is fixed and you've delegated most of the ongoing tasks. *Now* you can put your feet back up on the desk and do some strategic planning.

13

When Things Go Wrong: Handling the Difficult Employee

It is growing dark on a grey winter afternoon. It will be totally dark by the time you leave work. You stare out at the company parking lot, which is as bleak as you feel. The monthly summary must be finished tonight. Again you shuffle through the reports turned in by your subordinates, hoping that somehow Ronald Smith's report on his department, financial reconciliations, will magically become acceptable. Nothing, of course, happens. With a sigh you pick up the phone to call Ronald. Sue, Ronald's lead agent, reminds you that Ron called in sick yesterday and hasn't yet returned to work. She will try to find the information you need, but she's not sure she can make sense out of Ronald's files. Silently agreeing that Ron's files are a disaster, you ask her to try.

Later that evening, after completing the summary—with some guesswork in the financial reconciliations area—you try to decide what to do about Ronald Smith. While not a genius, he seems to have about average intelligence—when he applies it. He is marginally competent. When you were promoted to your current position, Ron was already in place as a supervisor; he has been with the company in that capacity for about two years. Since you took over, realizing that Ron was a weak supervisor, you've given him a lot of time and coaching. You always spend extra time with him when setting his yearly objectives and doing his performance appraisal. When you have corrected his work in the past, he has always been defensive. You have been particularly careful to notice when he performs above standard, and you have rewarded his few accomplishments with recognition to the best of your ability and budget. His work improves for a while, but always gets sloppy again.

He's also sick too often. It is hard to tell whether he really has a weak constitution or whether he takes short holidays. He never quite pushes it far enough to give you cause to fire him. Certainly he sounds sick when he calls, and he always regales the entire office with masterly descriptions of his recently departed miseries when he returns.

Just last month—one Friday evening—you had a long chat with Ron to discuss his performance, to be sure there were no problems you didn't know about, and to offer your assistance. Ron seemed uneasy and didn't really give you anything to work with. You took him for a drink afterward, hoping he might relax and open up. Aside from learning a few new jokes, the time was unproductive.

Mr. Smith will be back in the next few days. What are you going to do about the shoddy monthly report?

The marginal employee is one of the most complicated problems faced by the middle manager. It is easier (not easy but easy-*er*) and less draining to deal with a totally incompetent employee. You can document the incompetence according to the rules of your organization and then fire or demote the employee. (Always consider demotion as an option. If you handle it with understanding and support—and the employee is capable of the new position—it can benefit both sides. The company keeps the training and experience already invested in the employee, and the employee has a job that he or she can handle.) The marginally competent employee offers no such easy choices. Ron Smith's department has been meeting most of its goals, and the backlog hasn't increased. On the other hand, it hasn't decreased, either, which you rather hoped it might have by now. You decide that Ron's overall performance must be judged as adequate—just adequate. His personnel record shows that he has taken 13 sick days this year in groups of two and three.

You have several options. You may:

● Begin the documentation process (formal documentation that may be used to show why someone should be fired).

- Handle each of Ron's problems individually.
- Ignore the problems and focus on those things he does well—showing your confidence in him.

You decide to tackle Ron's problems individually, although you will also use elements of the other two solutions as well. You set up an informal documentation file on Mr. Smith and resolve to use both carrot and stick. For the carrot, you will take care to praise Ron's work when he deserves it. In the meantime, you prepare to apply the stick. You leave a note on his desk asking him to call for an appointment the day he returns. You review the last three monthly summaries Ron submitted noting all of the deviations from standard. You also update your old memo giving the requirements for monthly summaries and have it retyped. In this way, you will have specific examples of the inadequate work and the standards which apply to that work so both you and the employee can judge future efforts.

It snows all day Friday, the day Ron returns to work. You're half-exasperated at the employees who keep surreptitiously coming to see if they will be let out early, while you half-hope there *will* be a snow day so you can get to the ski slopes before the crowds. Because Mr. Smith rubs you wrong personally, you take five minutes before his appointment to relax and get a firm hold on your temper. True to your mental prediction, Ron's first question—on behalf of his staff, of course, he wants you to understand (!)—is how soon the company will be sending everyone home. Then he takes great pains to tell you about his wife's chicken soup which really helped him shake the flu and get back to work sooner. When you point out that he has missed 13 days of work this year, he gives you a pained expression and says he has a weak constitution. Besides, with the wife's new chicken soup recipe, he assures you, there won't be any further problem. And Sue can always fill in for him.

With a quiet sigh, you review the company policy on sick time. You also assign him the task of reviewing all of his files with his supervisors so they can find things in his absence. You then turn to the shoddy reports, reviewing specifically the problems in each. Ron doesn't seem to be listening very carefully, and he has more creative excuses than you thought possible: he was getting sick, his supervisors didn't have the right information, you have given him other assignments which took priority, etc. You take brief notes and discuss his excuses one at a time. You remind him the summary is one of his key deliverables. He quickly assures you that everything is okay, and that you'll have no more trouble. Privately, you think he just wants to get out of your office. You review the standards and tell him that you expect a perfect summary next month. Ron leaves in a hurry.

Whenever you review a performance problem with an employee be sure to ask for his or her ideas about what the problem is. Of course, you will have your own ideas as well. The employee may have very good reasons which you should address. The employee, like Ronald, may also have lots of excuses. It is important that you deal with these one at a time. If you don't, the employee will continue to use them.

There are many, many reasons why employees do not perform at the desired level. A good way to approach the problem is to think about what might prevent the employee from doing his or her job well. The employee may not have the skills or the strength. The environment might be wrong, or the proper tools may be lacking. The employee may not understand what he or she is supposed to do. There may be tremendous peer pressure against performing well. ("If you work too hard, it makes the rest of us look bad.") Chart 13.1 lists a series of questions to consider when faced with work that is below standard.

Two weeks later, while you are traveling on business, Ron calls you at the hotel late one night. He is furious. One of his lead agents, Bruce Patton, passed around a rather crude memo obviously intended to be a satire on Ron, you, and the company. It isn't funny and has stirred up considerable anger and hostility among the staff. Ron wants your permission to force Bruce to circulate a memo of apology . . . "and if he won't, I want to fire him. I want your support. This is totally unprofessional behavior and reflects badly on me."

YOU: Relax for a minute. Let's think this through.

RON: You mean you won't support me. If I can't fire people who are insubordinate and unprofessional, there's no point in my being a supervisor.

YOU: Ron, stop. Of course, you will have my support should firing be necessary.

RON: You mean after all I've said, you don't think we should get rid of Bruce? You were in the memo, too.

CHART 13.1

RESOLVING PERFORMANCE DIFFICULTIES

Ask yourself the following questions when confronted by poor performance:

1. Is the employee physically and mentally capable of doing the job?
    If not, help the employee get another job. No amount of motivation will overcome an inability to do the job.
2. Does the employee know *what* he or she is supposed to be doing?
    If not, review job descriptions, standards and objectives with the employee.
3. Does the employee have the right tools and equipment?
    If not, provide them. If money is tight, ask your employees to help with inexpensive solutions—they will often be surprisingly creative.
4. Is the physical working environment adequate?
    - Is it warm or cool enough?
    - Is the noise level too high?
    - Is there enough space for the working tools—and for working?
    If not, fix the problem. Here again, your staff may be able to help.
5. Does the employee know how to do the task?
    If not, arrange for training.
6. Does the employee remember how to do the task?
    If not, arrange for refresher training or reference materials. Particularly for jobs done very rarely, job aids and reference materials are more cost-effective than retraining.
7. Is the employee punished in some way for doing the job—or is there another activity that is more rewarding? (For instance, if every time your subordinates call in to report, you dump work on them, they will soon stop calling.)
    If so, try to eliminate the punishment.
8. Is good performance recognized and reinforced?
    If not, institute rewards. Be careful, however, you don't start something you can't carry on.

Employees can and generally want to help with problems. Let them help you. They actually *do* the jobs and often have figured out a better way to do them.

YOU: I'm not happy about it but it's not the first time. I seem to remember you rated Bruce as an outstanding supervisor in September?

RON: Yeah, I can't believe he was this stupid.

YOU: Well Bruce is pretty young. Maybe this is an area in which he needs some coaching. As to firing him, do you have anyone else ready to become a lead agent?

RON: No. I guess I can't spare him right now, but. . . .

After you finally get Ronald off the phone, you make a note to meet with him as soon as you return to counsel him about overreacting. The incident was somewhat serious, but not of the magnitude that would warrant an immediate firing. It should have been handled informally by Ron. When you return, you find that he's home sick again. Obviously the chicken soup didn't work.

Just before you meet with Ron again, your boss calls to say your trip to Lincoln has been delayed because of the weather. You can use the time in the office and are feeling good when your secretary announces that Ronald Smith is here for the meeting you requested. You begin by reviewing your meeting with Bruce Patton, indicating that you think Bruce won't repeat his satirical mistake. Ron is still annoyed and belligerent that you didn't agree stronger action was called for. You spend about half an hour discussing the need to manage each employee differently. Ron listens and nods his head, but you're not at all sure he agrees with you. You mention that there is no such thing as *the* right answer to a management problem, only solutions that have varying degrees of success. You are beginning to believe that one of Ron's problems is rigidity—an overdependence on black-and-white rules. You move on to discuss Ron's hasty temper and his overreaction to any challenge to his authority. After maintaining that strong rules are necessary to control staff members, Ron drops out of the conversation. You find yourself conducting a monologue except when you ask direct questions. You decide to conclude the meeting without discussing sick time or the now-growing backlog of investigations. Perhaps Ron will be more receptive next time. You remember to compliment him on the recently completed audit of his area and, as he is leaving, you ask how the monthly summary is coming along. Not meeting your eyes, he assures you the report is "hunky dory." You consider starting formal documentation, but decide to wait for the monthly summary.

Don't take on too much in a corrective meeting. No one can correct 500 things at once! You can usually, if you observe voice tone and body language, see when the employee has had enough. This is not to suggest that you let mistakes pass forever because the employee isn't ready to hear about them. Just be careful of overload. It doesn't get you where you want to go.

You turn away from the window where you have been looking at the dirty snow piled in the parking lot, wondering if winter will ever end. Ronald Smith's monthly summary doesn't herald spring either. There is marked improvement, but it still isn't right. You weigh his performance: the satisfactory audit was a commendable achievement; he has now missed 16 days from sickness (or impromptu vacations); he was the first supervisor to complete the documentation of his procedures and they were well done; he continues to make too much out of his authority. . . . In short, he is still only marginally adequate and is not improving as fast as he should after two meetings. What do you do now?

- Begin the formal documentation process?
- Continue to handle Ron's problems individually?
- Keep his performance difficulties a secret and try to transfer him somewhere else? (Don't laugh, far too many managers do this.)
- Acknowledge his performance problems and work with him to find a position to which he is better suited?

You decide once again to exercise several options. You discuss Ron with your boss and personnel emphasizing that he is very good technically. They promise to be on the lookout for a position that might better suit him. In the meantime, you plan to begin the formal documentation process with a first (oral) warning. Unfortunately, Ron's performance improves for a short period of time and then falls off again. You continue with the documentation process. Had his performance improved and stayed at a satisfactory level, you would have stopped the process at that point. (Many employees who go two and three steps into the documentation process do turn around and become average and even above-average performers. Some become successful managers. Guard against prejudice in this area.)

If your organization does not have guidelines for documentation, you can use a variant of the rules listed below, adapted to your circumstances.

1. Correct mistakes as you would for any employee. Make sure your corrections are specific and take place as soon as possible after the errors are made. Be sure to keep records of your actions. (Informal notes are fine.) Be sure the employee knows how to judge his or her own work according to standard and that the employee has the necessary skills and tools to do the job. Take extra care never to socially isolate an employee or group of employees you are correcting.

2. If the work continues to be below standard, meet with the employee to discuss the problem. Review the standards and specific examples of work that did not meet them. Take action to remove any excuses (valid or invalid) the employee mentions. Issue an informal (oral) warning to the employee that his or her performance must improve. Tell the employee you are making a note of this meeting and that you will meet again in three weeks to review the

"Listen! I don't care what your doctor said! You can't dress that way here!!"

employee's progress. Also tell him or her that you will be making formal and informal observations during the three weeks. Be especially careful to recognize good performance during this time.

3. If the work continues to be below standard, at the next meeting issue a formal written warning. List the specific problems and the standards the employee must reach to attain a satisfactory rating. Review the warning with the employee and ask the employee to sign your file copy indicating he or she received it. (You may wish to include wording that states the employee's signature indicates he or she received the warning not that he or she agrees with it. Employees will be more likely to sign in this case.) At this meeting, review the consequences if the employee continues to fall below standard:

- A record of this and all subsequent meetings will be placed in the employee's personnel file.
- You will meet again in three weeks. If the employee is still below standard, you will issue a final warning.
- Two weeks after the final notice, you will be forced to fire him or her if his or her work is not satisfactory.

Many companies choose this time to freeze all salary actions, delaying them until the employee improves. Be certain you don't *create* a failure by giving up on the employee. (If you expect someone to fail, he or she almost certainly will. This Cinderella effect works for success, too, which is one of the reasons why it behooves you to believe in your staff.)

4. The final-warning meeting is the time to let it all hang out. You and the employee both stand to lose a lot if this meeting doesn't result in improved performance. With all the patience and strength you can muster, review the performance deviations from the standard. Problem solve with the employee. Again, document the interview and ask the employee to sign it. Close with the reminder that this is the last warning: the employee has two weeks to clean up his or her act or face termination.

5. If the employee's improvement isn't satisfactory, fire him or her. Unless there are very unusual circumstances, insufficient improvement does *not* warrant retaining the employee. You've already worked at the problem for eight weeks! Don't prolong the agony.

Of course, these guidelines should be applied differently to different levels of employees. Poor managerial performance may reflect a poor style fit, in which case a transfer may be the solution. It is better for you as well as the employee if you can save a poor performer. It increases the loyalty and feelings of security of your staff and makes them work even harder for you. And it saves you the time and expense of hiring and training replacements.

Bad Apples Can Turn into Good Peaches

Be careful not to label people as failures. Documentation helps you to *reform* as well as to remove; of the two, reformation is preferable. It is particularly important, therefore, to recognize a turnaround in performance.

If your staff member's level and quality of work improves, stop the documentation process. (Many companies recommend holding the documentation records for a period of time in case of a reversion to earlier patterns—six months is common—and then, if everything is all right, destroying them so that future supervisors will not be unduly influenced.) Do reinforce the employee's good work but don't continue to single him or her out for special attention. Go on as if the documentation had never happened. Employees are entitled to a normal work life when they are performing satisfactorily. That way, you both reap the rewards of better performance.

Biting the Bullet

Well, it may finally be spring outside but it certainly isn't spring in your heart. Nothing has worked. The pattern of some short-term improvement followed by a return to inadequate performance has continued. Today, after four months of struggling, you are firing Ron. Your stomach is upset, and you wish you were someplace else— anyplace else.

It shouldn't be a surprise to Ron as you've followed the documentation process thoroughly. Nonetheless, it makes you even more uncomfortable to know that Ron thinks you are being unfair. You have, nevertheless, been as just as you know how. Your boss and the personnel manager have approved the termination papers and reviewed the last four months in detail. Ronald has met with personnel several times. It certainly isn't fair to Ron's staff to continue to employ a poor supervisor.

No one (except sickies) enjoys firing someone, especially people who are supporting families, but there are times the job demands it. It is unfair to people who *do* work hard at their jobs to continue to employ—and pay—someone who doesn't.

There are arguments as to what the best (kindest) time of day and day of the week for firing are. Some people opt for Friday afternoon at quitting time, reasoning that the employee has the whole weekend to come to grips with the situation. Others pick a time earlier in the week, the assumption being that the employee can immediately begin picking up the pieces, looking for a new job, etc. The situation—or company policy—will often dictate your choice.

In this case, you have decided to release Ron on a Thursday, about three-thirty in the afternoon. You will hold a meeting immediately afterward to announce to the staff that Ronald Smith has been fired and to state briefly that he was fired for thoroughly recorded and discussed performance problems. You take the force out of the rumor mill by making the announcement immediately and make the rest of the staff feel secure by telling them that Smith had plenty of warning. (See Chart 13.2 for a sample script for such a staff meeting.) After the staff meeting, you schedule time to compose yourself. You will give Ron the choice of leaving right away—cleaning his desk out that night or on the weekend—or staying the rest of the day and cleaning out his desk about the time people are leaving for home. He can also visit personnel on Friday without having to wait the entire weekend.

Before beginning a termination interview, be sure you have followed all the rules your organization may have about firings. Your company may require an exit interview with personnel or may insist

CHART 13.2

SAMPLE SCRIPT TO ANNOUNCE A FIRING

FOCUS	EXAMPLE
State Purpose	I've called you together to let you know that I have fired Ron Smith.

Give a brief reason(s)	Firing someone is a serious matter and I want you to know that Ron had ample opportunity to clean up his act. We went through the entire documentation process, which takes about four months. Ron has been performing below the standards for his position for some time. Over the last six months, he and I discussed his productivity frequently and we documented his performance in order to be sure he was given a fair chance.
Give assurance	Ron was not meeting his objectives. I want to assure each of you that your own evaluations are based on the actual work completed.
Restate standards	You each know the standards and objectives set for your areas. You should, therefore, be able to measure your own performance.
List ways to solve problems	If you have questions about the standards or your own performance, please see your supervisor or me. We're available to work on problems with you, as is personnel should you feel uncomfortable speaking with us.
Handle the transition	We will, of course, be replacing Ron in the next few weeks. His position will be posted for applications on Thursday. In the meantime, Sue and Ray will report to Glynne temporarily.
Handle other small items if appropriate	By the way, the new spring rates will become effective on Friday. Please be sure to review the new rates release by then.
Answer questions	Are there any questions?
Reiterate assurance	When someone is fired, sometimes others become insecure. Once again, I would like to assure you that if you are performing satisfactorily, you should have no fears about your job security.
Conclusion	It is upsetting to lose Ron but we now need to get on with our work. Thank you.

that someone from personnel be present at the interview (mostly as a witness to protect you). Try to be as relaxed as you can be before you begin. Use some of the stress-reduction methods listed in Chapter 2. It probably won't be pleasant, but it is a part of your job. You do no one—especially yourself—a service by retaining incompetent staff. Get ready (make sure you won't be disturbed and have some tissues handy), then just do it.

It should be an extremely rare occurance when a firing does not follow the pattern of Ronald Smith's. It is almost *never* the right thing to fire someone on the spot. The strangest of circumstances can sometimes have an innocent explanation. It is hard, for example, to think of a valid reason for someone having a hand in the till; still, take enough time, without evading the situation, to validate the facts. If you work in a union situation or with employment contracts know the rules before you start. You'll save yourself a lot of grief and the possibility of being forced to rehire someone—difficult and embarrassing to say the least.

Senior management personnel may have certain benefits extended to them by the company, such as outplacement counseling, the use of an office for a limited time, etc. Again, make sure you know and are prepared to tell the employee what rights he or she has.

There is no perfect way to start a termination interview. You might begin like this:

Ron, I'm sorry to say that, as we discussed last week, your performance has not improved sufficiently, and I must let you go. Today is your last day.

Pause here but go on as soon as you can.

You receive three weeks' severence pay plus the seven days remaining unused vacation you have. I have a check for that amount plus your pay for the last two weeks.

Please give me your identification card and your company credit card. As soon as I receive all of the company-owned materials you have, I will give you your final check. Your benefits terminate in two weeks.

Should you have any questions about your benefits, please call Timothy Team in personnel.

It is most unlikely you'll get it all out that neatly. So make sure you have a list of things that must be covered.

Being fired brings out different reactions in different people. Some cry; others get angry and threaten you or the company; still others (by far the most difficult to take) beg you to take them back. However difficult the situation may be, don't change your mind. It is to be hoped that you have followed the documentation process and have carefully weighed the situation *before* arriving at this point. On-the-spot emotion clouds the issue.

If you have been diligent in coaching and prodding the employee while you still hoped for reformation, and you have followed the documentation process completely—with all the built-in opportunities for the employee to improve—chances are there will be no sudden reformation, the employee will repeat the failures that led to the decision to terminate, and you will find yourself firing him or her all over again. Don't prolong the agony and, especially, don't bargain. Chances are it won't work for either side.

In the face of anger or tears, stay as calm as you can. Don't return threats or continue responding to complaints about you or the company. Refer to your list to keep you on track and conclude the interview as soon as possible. If the employee leaves before you conclude (it is not unknown for a fired employee to walk out on you in the middle of the interview), arrange for the personnel department (or a neutral party) to complete the process and turn over the final paycheck and severance monies (if any). Do try to remember that your former employee is a human being and is more upset than you are!

Finally, even if the employee has rights of notice or will receive an office and outplacement assistance under a contract (or some other requirement that will delay the actual moment the employee leaves the company), get the employee out of your department *immediately*. Most people who have been fired find it embarrassing and will leave quickly. Some, however, will linger to help or cause trouble. In either case, a fired employee hanging around will be a disruption to the workday no matter how well behaved he or she may be. No one wants to work with a ghost. If you have to arrange for him or her to be given office space somewhere else in the building, do so. Just get the gloom out of your area.

Ron has gone for the moment, slamming the door behind him. You stare unseeing at his file for a few minutes. Then, after taking a few deep breaths, you hold a short staff meeting about Ron. Coming back to your office, you ask your secretary to hold your calls for a bit. You feel cold and your stomach is churning. You're depressed and upset and, honestly, relieved that he's gone. You pick up the phone and arrange to play racquetball with a friend that evening. The exercise will help you get the bad taste out of your mouth.

Don't let yourself brood over a firing. Only the very callous—who generally make poor managers anyway—are not upset by firing someone. You probably won't feel much like celebrating, but do *something* to take your mind off the day's events. Save something you enjoy doing and can work on by yourself to give you time to relax; your staff will probably be avoiding you in any case. Then the evening after you must fire someone, try to arrange to do something to help release the stress, such as a hard physical workout or fast athletic game, dinner at a luxurious restaurant, or a funny movie. You've done what you had to do; now it's time to get refreshed so you can plunge back into the fray.

The first time you fire someone is the worst. It never gets easy, but like anything else you learn from experience. Most people are angry, shocked, and hurt when they are fired. More than a few have said, looking back at it, that it became a turning point in their lives: that they got their lives together, changed professions, were ultimately better off for it. Not everyone will feel that way, of course. Nonetheless people work for their wages. When that implied contract isn't fulfilled on either side, it should be terminated. When it is the employee who fails to earn his or her salary—and continues to do so after attempts have been made to correct the situation—a manager has no option except to fire.

The Difficult Employee Who Isn't Inadequate

But what about employees who are difficult to handle but who are also good performers? (The classic example is the research scientist who produces wonderful results but is a fussy prima donna. Things are expected to be done his or her way and no other—and nothing is ever likely to change those habits.) Clearly, if they're good performers you want to have them around to help you meet your objectives, but if they cause problems, you have to do something about them.

It depends on what makes the person difficult. Each case will be different. Start by thinking about what makes the employee hard to deal with and what motivates the employee to act in that manner. (See Chapter 12.) If, for example, the employee needs attention, don't reward outrageous acts by giving it to him. Recognize and reward only that behavior you want to have repeated while looking for showmanship tasks to delegate to him. If the employee is exactly the opposite and hides under her desk every time senior management comes to visit, assign jobs that require gradually increasing amounts of personal contact. If the difficulty lies in the fact that the employee is intimidating and has a stronger style than you do, remember that you are the boss. Remain assertive rather than aggressive, and don't compete with your employee. If you just can't stand the employee's personality, learn to grin and bear it. It was never a part of a manager's job to love every employee.

The important thing to remember is that you want good performers. They are the key to your continuing career growth. As long as the difficult but productive employee can be kept under control, you should work at it. Only when the results produced are outweighed by the difficulties he or she causes should you begin the documentation process.

It is, after all, part of management to deal with difficult situations as well as easy ones.

14

Stop the World, I Want to Get Off: Managing Change

After accepting his metaphorical watch at a retirement dinner recently, a spry white-haired manager spoke about the changes that had taken place during his 40 year career: from the first commercial airline flights to a man on the moon. He mentioned the astounding efficiencies made possible by the first photocopying machines and his even greater delight with the "magic" of the electronic mail terminal recently installed in his old office. Younger managers in the audience nodded sagely and commented to each other how wonderful it was that Harry kept his mind alert and accepted change so well. He would get along well in retirement—probably be the first on his block to buy a home computer. Good old Harry, they said as they went home, we wish our employees would accept change as well as he does.

Meanwhile Harry gathered together the parting gifts from a corporation in which he had invested a large part of his life. His wife picked up his briefcase and said, because she thought she must, that the dinner had been nice and the speeches most complimentary about Harry's contributions. Harry smiled fondly, but couldn't help adding sadly that Mary, his division head, must have done a lot of research in order to have known anything much about him. She'd only been his boss for three weeks. He had had seven managers in the last 18 months.

It wasn't the changing machines that bothered him, Harry said, it was the constantly changing people. No one even had a chance to get to know each other any more. He looked at the engraved plaque and told himself it wasn't his problem anymore. All the same, he wondered how the young supervisors he knew would be able to keep up with the geometrically increasing rate of change. Would they know anyone at all at their retirement dinners? Would there even be retirement dinners to mark this very human rite of passage? He took his wife's arm and started for home.

Change is a major part of life today. Accumulated knowledge and access to that knowledge *is* increasing geometrically. By the time the general public becomes aware of a new theory or technology, it is often already old by research and production standards and frequently obsolete. In rapidly moving fields such as data processing, professionals who leave positions in the mainstream for as little as a year find themselves quite out of date. They are no longer on the cutting edge of their field, and their knowledge is obsolete.

Even in fields less fast moving, the quest to stay up to date can be difficult. As the Red Queen said to Alice, you have to run as fast as you can in order to stay in the same place. If you learn to adapt easily, it will help your career. If you don't, you may find yourself in a dead-end, without the skills necessary to be promoted.

Throughout history, knowledge and information—and the ability to apply them—have translated directly into profits. In the 19th century, London tea merchants posted lookouts along the English Channel and maintained teams of couriers to bring the information gleaned to their headquarters. A good lookout often made the company's fortune, for the arrival of the first clipper ships of the season, loaded with tea from China, would have a drastic effect on market prices in London. An inventory worth a fortune one day could be worth a fraction of that the next. Today, business is less dependent on lookouts and couriers, but information is still its lifeblood. A few large corporations have now gone so far as to have their own *internal* satellite communications systems, so vital has the rapid transfer of information become. The survivors, corporate and individual, have demonstrated that they can both adapt to changing circumstances and also use those changing circumstances to advantage.

Before you can help others, you must be able to help yourself. When you recognize that you will be facing a period of unusual change, take as many of the steps listed below as seem to apply to your situation. The object is to orient yourself so that you are ready for the additional work that will be needed, so that you are as personally comfortable with the anticipated changes as possible, and so that you will have some stress-reduction outlets set up in advance.

Step 1

Begin by thinking through the anticipated change sometime when you are very relaxed. You may want to use a pad to jot down the answers to these questions.

- What changes do you expect?

- How good are your sources of information? How can you improve them?

- What is the best thing that could happen to you as a result of the anticipated changes? The worst?

- What additional (or reduced) responsibilities will you have as a result of the change? How will the changes affect your staff?

Step 2

Come to terms with yourself. Decide now (or within a reasonable time) what *you* will be doing. For example, if your division is moving to Salt Lake City, are you going to ask to transfer, or will you remain where you are? If you will remain where you are, how long will you stay with your current organization before you start looking for a new position? If you are not at peace with yourself, you will waste lots of time and create a lot of unnecessary personal stress making and remaking these decisions. Your decision is not cast in concrete, of course, but a decision frees you to do other things. If you're very insecure, you can't work well. (By the way, if you do your job very well during a period of high change, you will shine. Many of your colleagues will be falling apart at the seams. A period of high change can be very good for your career.)

Step 3

Organize yourself to the nth degree. Create forms, set up files, enlist your secretary's help, appoint a chief of staff if you don't have one. Free yourself of as many of the daily demands as you can. You almost can't be too organized, as long as all of the elements of your planning allow for changes to the changes.

Step 4

Set up regular ways of reducing stress. Get and take vitamins if you don't now; eat right; book and pay for some sports activity. (If you pay for it in advance, you're more likely to do it.) Plan a small amount of personal time each day so you have at least five minutes that are yours. Arrange to do things you enjoy and which give you energy.

Step 5

Tell your family and friends about what you expect. This is not the same as taking your job home. If you expect to work extra hard or to have significiant changes take place in your career or working habits (even if it just means that you will be more tired), your friends and family will be involved. If they understand what is going on, they will feel more secure and will be able to help create a better haven for you. (Don't use this as an excuse to dump on those who are important to you, but acknowledge that the people who care about you do have a right to try to help.)

Step 6

Think through the ramifications of the change for your staff members and start collecting the information you will need to help your staff deal with the changes.

Step 7

Plan and replan. Make contingency plans for everything you can think of. Things *will* go wrong. Allow lots of time for anticipated problems.

Step 8

Expect the change to be constant. It is crucial that you understand that even when you are sure everything is final, *something* will change. It will be easier to handle if you expect it.

But, you say, this is all advance work, sometimes you don't know anything about major changes until you are in the middle of them. Quite true, which only empasizes two things: (1) the better organized you are as a manager, the more you can take advantage of unexpected changes, and (2) it is very important that you maintain good sources of information. Major change can come from very unexpected sources. A short rewording of a governmental regulation can revolutionize your industry. A conglomerate can purchase your organization. A chemist working in another country can create a cheaper substitute for your major product. Your boss can quit to take another position. Chart 14.1 lists some of the areas you might consider when evaluating what might influence your organization.

CHART 14.1

YOUR CRYSTAL BALL: SOME AREAS TO WATCH FOR CHANGE

Within Your Organization
- Management
  - —People
  - —Style
- Work force
  - —People
  - —Skill or education level
  - —Demands
- Location (relocations)
- Products or services produced

Outside Your Organization
- Economic up or downturn
- Legislative or regulatory moves
- Political
  - —People
  - —Method of government
- Competitors
- Customer needs and values
- Technology
  - —Energy sources
  - —Communications
  - —Transportation
  - —Information storage and access
  - —Manufacturing methods
  - —Agribusiness methods

Boss, The Sky Is Falling! Chicken Little Revisited

Managing a staff for high productivity during a time of high change is rather like juggling uncooked eggs. The rumor mill goes into overdrive; you will hear "facts" that make the sky falling seem tame. Your staff members will be as much or more concerned than you are about your respective fates. What can you do to keep your staff members happy and productive?

The most important element is to communicate: first, last, and in between. Overcommunicate. Increase the frequency of your staff meetings and be sure that you are accessible to your employees for individual conferences. (You may want to set up formal office hours when employees know you will be available to speak with them—similar to those set by college professors.)

People are more secure when they know what is going on and believe that they are as current as possible. This does NOT mean that you should give your staff material that is confidential, or that you should tell them things you are sure will soon change. Just as you work better when you are reasonably secure, they will produce better when they feel that they are in control of their lives. It may happen during staff meetings that you are asked to give information that you do not wish to give. Depending upon the circumstances, you may wish to use an answer similar to this one:

Although there has been a tentative decision made in this area, we believe that it is likely to change. Rather than give you an answer which may cause you to base your plans on something I'm not sure will happen, I would rather not give you an answer now. As soon as I have reliable information, I will be sure to communicate with you.

The success of this type of answer depends upon the degree of trust your staff has in you. Don't give information too early (it loses its effectiveness, and your staff may spend too much time worrying and too little time working) or too late (it doesn't allow your staff to plan properly). It is a judgment call. The rate of change during a major project is unevenly paced; sometimes accelerating, sometimes slowing down. The better your sense of timing, the more effectively you will manage during change.

Be especially careful of things you promise your staff. You will lose or at least sour an employee each time you must renege on a promise.

During periods of high change you may not be able to provide promotional opportunities, for example, that you could at other times.

It is important that you employ all of your skills as a manager in motivating your staff during periods of uncertainty. Maintain all of the recognition programs you have in place and give special kudos to those who go beyond the normal demands. At the same time review the standards from time to time and be sure to institute disciplinary actions when appropriate. Don't fire out of hand or from accumulated stress but do fire for incompetence or for lack of productivity. Update and modify objectives when necessary so that your employees cannot hide behind the changing environment. Be even more observant than usual. Look, listen, and learn what your staff is really doing.

Before You Go to Turkey Lurkey, Examine the Piece of Sky That Fell on You

Stopping the scare rumors can be one of the most important contributions you and your staff can make to the organization. It is almost an axiom: the higher the rate of change, the wilder and more unsettling the rumors. People love to gossip and to scare themselves, hence ghost stories and rumors. Ask your staff to become rumor stoppers. Tell them that if they will bring you all of the latest rumors (without attribution—you're after the rumor not the person), you will check them out as far as you can and let them know what you find out. Then do it. They will spend less time fussing and more time meeting your objectives.

The most useful thing you can do for your employees is to provide some lubrication between them and the organization. Try not to pass on stress and shield them from whatever ill effects the change creates. At the same time, give them as much support as you can and they will reward you with loyalty and productivity.

Making the Most of the End of the World

Periods of change are periods of opportunity for both you and your staff members. During high change, others—some who were not perhaps as prepared as you were—will resign, get reassigned, relocate, in any case, move. You and your staff may also be forced to make decisions: whether or not to adjust to a new management style, to accept a new position, to relocate, to find a new job. Is this what you really want to be doing? Many people fall into a job and stay there forever, perhaps not hating it but not loving it either. Change is frequently uncomfortable—but, if you must make a change, why not make the best possible one for you? Take the time to think your life through and encourage your employees to do the same. While not always pleasant, these decisions can become the basis of a personal life review. Change, if you let it, gives you (and your staff, of course) the excuse to examine your life.

Life AFTER Change

Change is a time of high risk and high reward. Without it we could never grow or learn. If you can learn to use it to your advantage, you will have an asset to your upward mobility. If you are properly prepared, it can also be great fun.

15

Can We Be Friends? Ethics and Responsibility for the Manager

What should you do if you are asked to do something you consider unethical and you can't afford to quit? If everyone else is really doing it, can you refuse to conform without being a prig? What will your behavior do to your career? When push comes to shove, where does your loyalty lie? With management? With your staff? In your own best interest? And where is that?

If you decide on the unethical approach, when do you draw the line? How do you handle your employees infractions of the rules? (This is sometimes called the expense-report question. Doesn't everyone cheat just a little? If so, when does creative accounting stop?)

Do you give full pay to an employee who is missing work because her spouse is dying? Is the answer the same for the death of a significant other (such as a live-in boyfriend or girlfriend)? Does the answer change if the employee has been with the company for 23 years or only three months? Do you treat the situation differently for the employee who worked late and on Saturdays than you do for the employee who left precisely at five every day?

Can you be friends with your manager? With the people on your staff? If so, what do you do when a friend performs poorly? Does the situation change if you know there are extenuating circumstances?

How about more than friends? How do affairs with your employees affect your ability to manage—and your career? (Even if you think it is totally secret, it isn't. You may think you are the exception; you aren't.)

Shades of Gray

There aren't any right answers to these questions, but there are most certainly wrong ones. Answers that can ruin your career and get you fired. Answers that can destroy other lives. Answers that can cause suicides.

Why raise these questions, then, if there are no correct answers? Because it is helpful to have considered them, even abstractly; and because awareness will help you to understand the potential ramifications of your actions; because careers built on integrity last longer and are more rewarding than those built on deception.

And because as a manager you are responsible for the results of your decisions.

Some random thoughts based on the hard-won experiences of others are listed below; they may help you clarify your thinking.

- The manner in which you do your daily work affects the performance of your employees. They see much more than you may think.

- Friendship does muddy the waters. Whether or not to be real friends with your employees is a personal decision. If you do become friends, you must guard against partiality and you lay yourself open for increased personal pain in cases of poor performance.

- Although you are responsible for *your* actions, you cannot, even if you are chairman of the board, totally control a large corporation. Even in smaller organizations, no one's power is absolute. You are not responsible for everything that happens. (The concept of limited responsibility is an important one. It can save you from ulcers.)

- A hopeless crusade against a management policy that you know won't be changed does nothing for your employees and may hurt your career. It may even make your staff more difficult to manage. Why should they work hard to meet objectives set by people you obviously don't respect?

- When you continue to pay an employee who is not carrying his or her full weight, you are cheating everyone else who does earn every penny. You also cheat the stockholders. This problem carried to an extreme could put the entire company out of business. That means the loss of considerably more than the first job.

- Employees, except in unusual circumstances, are adults with responsibilities of their own and with *free will*. (If you employ teenagers, you will, of course, have some additional responsibilities resulting from the relative inexperience of your staff.)

- Everyone makes mistakes. It is better to admit a mistake straight away and to correct it. (Unless, of course, you make a mistake every hour—in which case the mistake you are making is that you are in the wrong job.)

In the case of managerial responsibility, the best defense is a good offense. Try to insure that you are never "in a box." If the ethical situation is impossible and you have another skill—or can apply your current skills in a new situation—and have enough money in the bank to cover the transition, you have the option of choosing a new situation. Frequently, just the knowledge that you have the option is sufficient to resolve the situation.

In light of this, then, what are the answers to the questions at the beginning of the chapter?

What *do* you do if asked to do the unethical and you can't afford to quit? You try to find a solution that accomplishes the same result but is not unethical. If that's impossible, consider doing the task. As far as it is possible, get instructions and directions in writing. (Sometimes that will make the problem go away. People are often reluctant to put such things in writing.) At the same time, start immediately to look for another job.

If it's illegal, and you can't find a legal way to accomplish what you're being asked to do, your only options are to do it, opening yourself to possible prosecution, or to quit. Resigning *is* an option.

Now, the expense-account question: when does creative accounting stop? There are three things to consider.

First, your environment: what's considered cheating in one company is recognized as a perk and a standard practice in another. Second, consider your own conduct. This is an area where you must conform to the rules you set for your employees. If you cheat, you must approve their cheating. And, third, you have to consider enforceability. You must enforce anything on which you take a stand. Conversely, there's no point in taking a stand when you know you will be unable to monitor and enforce that stand.

Should you cheat on your expense account? No.

Do you give full pay to an employee who is missing work because a spouse, significant other, friend, relative, etc. is dying? There are several considerations.

First, there's company policy. Some companies have a policy for such things. Going against that policy on your own is as dangerous as any other situation where you contravene company policy. If there is no policy (or it is vague), discuss the situation with your manager and personnel or benefits. Find out what has been done in the past. Remember, too, that work can help people take their minds off serious problems and provide some accomplishment during times of heavy stress, so giving time off may not be the most humane thing to do. Some jobs are also more flexible than others; an employee might be able to take work home or to the hospital—justifying your continuance of their pay.

How about individual situations? Employees who have given more *do* deserve extra consideration. If this is made clear to others, it can have a positive rather than a negative effect on the productivity of other staff members.

What about live-ins versus spouses? We are living in a time of cultural change. Bonds can be as strong or stronger outside of sanctioned relationship than in more formal ones. Nevertheless, whatever your preferences, you are not dispersing your own money. Therefore, you have a responsibility to consult with the managers of the organization for their preferences. You, of course, will present your case as effectively as you can.

There are no hard and fast rules or answers to these or any other business-ethics questions. Your responsibility lies in examining all the facts, determining as many options as possible, and then reviewing your obligations to your employees, yourself, and your employer. Bear in mind that you as a manager are paid to represent the interests of the shareholders. Whether you choose to continue representing their interests, as promulgated by senior management (especially in cases of illegal or unethical acts), is up to you. In the final analysis, you present your views, modify (if possible) harsh directives, and, as a last resort, quit. You must decide.

Think through your decisions as you make them. However difficult, it is ever so much easier before than after. In the grey land of managerial ethics, don't panic when you are faced with difficult decisions—but don't treat them lightly.

Parties? Bah Humbug!

A vice president of a major corporation mentions from time to time that he has become a Scrooge. He runs a fairly small shop of very creative people—some of them quite young. He hates birthdays and parties held by his employees. It seems that some years ago an office party was held for George's birthday and a group of staff members went out to lunch for Sally's birthday, but Henry's birthday was forgotten until a week after the fact. Henry's performance suffered. Later on, Loretta held a party, inviting the vice president and most, but not all, of the members of the department. When he declined the invitation because everyone was not invited, Loretta threw a fit and accused him of trying to run her personal life.

So he hates office-connected parties. His personal solution is to buy the same type of cake for each birthday in the office and to severely restrict his social engagements with employees outside the office.

Everything you do as manager has implications. You have the right, of course, to make friends among those on your staff, but remember too you may have to pay a price for what others may see as favoritism. Every member of your staff is an individual; every individual wants to be special, and you, as a manger, are a major factor in your staff members' lives.

Changing the World—Bit by Bit

If you don't like the world as it is today, you—the successful middle manager—can change it. You have the power and the responsibility to do the best with it you can. If you don't like the system, change your part of it.

If you work for 40 years rising to senior middle management, you will probably directly manage at least 60 managers and supervisors. They will, in their turn, manage 60 more. And so on.

You really do have the opportunity to influence the world of business. Start now with your own small piece. If you would like to see a healthier work environment, make the environment for your staff as healthy as you can. Teach your subordinate managers and supervisors to do the same. Instill in them the desire to reinstitute this healthy environment in every managerial position they hold throughout their careers.

It is nice to be able to call Singapore from New York, to fly from Munich to Toronto and be able to rent a car with a small piece of plastic, to buy contact lenses made out of a material that didn't exist three years ago, to buy and use a home computer, to live in the world today—a world maintained in large measure by business. It is your world, make of it what you will.

16

What's in It for Me?

Hire the best.
Pay them fairly.
Communicate frequently.
Provide challenges and rewards.
Believe in them.
Get out of their way—

they'll knock your socks off.

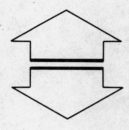

SECTION III

MANAGING LATERALLY

Introduction

*E*ven though they don't supervise you, and you don't supervise them, your peers are an important part of your working life. They are the managers and supervisors who are in positions parallel to your own; the people with the same or similar job titles to yours; the people to left and right of you on the organization chart.

Why do you need to manage them? Suppose you are the chief cook and bottle washer at The Down-in-the-Dumps Diner. You are supreme in your department, lord of all you survey. But you don't stand alone. You need a host of others working with you. If someone doesn't grow and ship food, there's nothing to cook. If someone·doesn't design advertising, no one comes to eat. If someone doesn't serve the food, there are no plates and bottles to wash. If someone doesn't set prices, collect monies due, pay suppliers, and keep books, there is no profit and no (gasp!) paycheck. And, if all that doesn't happen, The Down-in-the-Dumps Diner won't *need* a chief cook and bottle washer.

So even if you manage both up and down perfectly, there's still more to it. Somehow, you must deal successfully with all those other areas that are vital to the success of your own.

That's what managing laterally is all about.

17

Helping Your Peers to Help You: Get Your Full Share of Support

Because there is no reporting relationship involved, many middle managers forget to apply their management skills to their peers. Yet few jobs can be done without information, help, or approval from this group. This book, for example, had to be approved by an editorial committee before the editor could purchase it. Publishing a book is similar to producing a product in other businesses. During the course of publication, an editor must work with a series of peer departments: legal, advertising, art, sales, copyediting, production. An editor's relationship with these departments can make or break his or her product. They can do the same for you: peer departments and their managers can help you look great or can stonewall you without appearing to do so.

In addition, your peers can be a source of information and history—particularly valuable when you are taking over a new department. They can fill you in on "the way things are done around here" and shortcuts. They can tell you about the boss and other departments heads with whom you will have to work. They can forewarn you in times of crises; they can give you the latest rumors (very important when properly analyzed); they can help you in numerous ways. How do you help them to help you?

First, get to know them as colleagues and as people. What are their strengths and weaknesses? Who runs a tight ship? Who's the last person to complete his or her budget? As individuals, what do they find amusing? What do they do for fun? Do some on and off work socializing. Drop by to chat from time to time (being careful not to become a nuisance). Develop some genuine friendships if you can. Then apply some of the management skills that got you where you are: interactive listening, selling, team support, and positive reinforcement.

INTERACTIVE LISTENING

Listen as carefully to your peers as you do to your subordinates. The very act of focusing your whole attention on the speaker and listening completely encourages others to confide in you. You'll learn a lot about what is going on around you; it will all be helpful one way or another. (Just be careful your office doesn't become a convenient place for drop-ins with time on their hands to hang around.)

SELLING

From time to time, in a low-key manner, tell your peers about your accomplishments and successes. They will spread the news without even thinking about it. If they come to believe you are a successful manager, they will want to be associated with you and your projects. Everyone wants to work with a winner.

TEAM SUPPORT

Help other managers when they need it for three reasons:

- It is part of your job.

- The better your team does, the better it is for you. An atmosphere of success is pleasant to work in and tends to foster more success.

- When you need help, you will be able to collect your markers. Chances are, however, that you won't even need to mention your prior help. Your peers will probably help you willingly.

POSITIVE REINFORCEMENT

Let your peers know when you think they have done a good job. People appreciate and remember those who notice when they have worked extra long or hard on a project and done particularly well. Make it a point to write a well done to a peer every once in a while.

Negotiation: What You Do When You and Your Peers at Lonely Lumpit Cheeses, Inc., Don't Agree

You won't always agree with your peers on everything! When you don't, you need to be able to negotiate a reasonable compromise. Negotiation uses all of the skills already listed with the addition of compromise. Before you meet with someone for negotiations, prepare and plan carefully. Think the situation through. Where can you adjust your schedule or demands? Try to have several points of compromise. You can choose the most appropriate on the spot. If one is rejected, you can offer another. Then decide which points you absolutely cannot and will not concede and write them down. Review the past to see if the manager "owes" you anything from prior meetings or help you have given. Think over everything you know about this manager's personal style and decide what approach (hard or soft opening) you will take. Set up the meeting either on neutral or your territory. And as with any potentially stressful meeting, be sure that you are as relaxed as possible before you begin. Then, follow these steps:

1. Begin by affirming your commitment to the goals you must both meet. State that you are prepared to compromise and trust that the other party will do the same.

2. Review the situation—listing both the points of agreement and those of disagreement.

3. Offer your first concession. (Remember to sell by telling the manager what is in it for him or her.)

4. Ask for your peer to compromise in that area you most need or to offer another suggestion.

5. Continue back and forth until you have reached a compromise that is acceptable to both of you. Do *not* give up those points you listed as essential.

6. Review the agreement and summarize actions to be taken. Leave the meeting on a positive note, if possible.

7. Write a memo confirming the new agreement so there will be no future misunderstandings (on this topic, at least).

8. If you cannot reach agreement, try to set up another meeting with someone else present who can mediate. That person (or persons) may be a respected peer or your respective managers.

Chart 17.1 gives an example of these steps in use.

Sometimes *nothing* you can do will cause a peer to work with you. You may find it necessary to ask your boss to intervene. In particularly difficult cases, even your boss may have to go up the line. This will work, but there will be repercussions. Don't expect sunshine and light from someone on whom you've put organizational pressure. But, after all is said and done, your job is to get the work done—not to run a social club.

No one said this was going to be easy.

Dealing With Cherry Chump, the Most Difficult Manager at Lonely Lumpit Cheeses

You've only been on vacation for a week. You can't believe that Cherry has been able to wreak so much havoc during that time. You recognize that Cherry is the most difficult of your peers with whom you and your subordinates must deal. Although you recognize her financial skills in isolation, you privately think she couldn't manage her way out of a paper bag when there are people involved. She has brusquely delegated some secretarial tasks to your second in command; she has managed to alienate your major supplier who is now thinking about raising his prices; and she has, apparently, reported to your mutual boss that you are out of control. Gritting your teeth, you decide that your vacation is really over.

What can you do with a team member who doesn't, won't, or can't play ball? With more delicacy (as this person doesn't report to you) and more strength (sometimes power is the only thing that works), you apply the same type of carrot and stick you would to an employee. Take extra care to keep the lines of communication open. Reinforce positive behavior. Document your conversations and agreements more often than you do normally. (In more blunt terms, cover your ass more.) Don't be overruled, nor become obnoxious yourself. When you meet with peers such as this, make sure you have your information straight, then be assertive. Lay it right on the line. (Be careful never to accuse someone of something you can't prove.) Finally make sure that your managers and supervisors understand that they are to accept assignments and direction only from you (or those senior to you in your line of report). They can use a phrase similar to the following: "I'm sorry, but my manager has assigned me to several very important projects with critical delivery dates. I have been instructed not to

CHART 17.1

NEGOTIATING WITH PEERS

STEP	SAMPLE SCRIPT
1. **Affirm:** —commitment —willingness to compromise —confidence peer *will* compromise	1. Jerry, you and I are on the same team. We both want to get the government contract. In order to get there, I'm willing to make some compromises—and I'm sure you will, too.
2. **Review:** —agreements —disagreements	2. We both agree Ann is an excellent analyst who does good work. Ann currently has a number of assignments. I need her to continue doing her daily work. You feel she is the only person who can prepare the figures for the presentation and she should work full time on that for the next three weeks.
3. **Offer the first concession**	3. I've thought about it thoroughly and I can arrange for Fredericka to take over some of Ann's supervisory duties. Ann can devote the extra free time to supervising someone who prepares the analysis. That way we get the benefits of her expertise without taking her away from other necessary work.
4. **Ask for a concession**	4. Can you supply an analyst? Ann will provide the direction, supervise the work, and review the final figures.
5. **Continue to negotiate**	5. Offers and counter-offers are exchanged until you both agree.
6. **Review and summarize positively**	6. Well, I think we both agree that with Ann supervising Jennifer and Joe and with an interim and final review at which you and I are present, we'll get the figures we need. Thanks for your support.
7. **Write a confirming memo**	7. Be sure the memo lists everything you agreed upon and send copies to everyone involved—including your supervisors if appropriate.

accept any further assignments without first discussing them with her. I'll tell her about this task. I'm sure she'll be getting back to you shortly."

A Gold Mine in Disguise: Using Your Organization

Most companies, even small ones, have vast resources that are rarely tapped. If you can locate and use these areas, you can stretch your budget, improve your department's procedures, create more effective presentations, give out special (free) incentives to your staff, attend specialized courses, and much more.

The first step is to look at the organization chart, pick up the phone and ask. "Can you help me? I'd like to. . . ." Start with those departments whose names suggest that they offer the service you are seeking. If, for example, you want to have some help in prescreening applicants for a new position, call the personnel department. If you think your lead supervisor could use some help in developing more effective work-flow processes, call the methods and procedures department. (One note of caution, before you call an area that might be considered a watchdog area—one which will report all of your problems up the line and insist on staying to help you fix them *their* way—check the grapevine. There is no point in inviting trouble.) If your first call doesn't work, then try an area that does a lot of what you want to do. For instance, it may not be the training department's responsibility to create presentations for other areas, but you can bet they are experts at creating their own. A few words of honest flattery later, you may have some help in preparing your best presentation yet. Marketing almost always has literally thousands of giveaways with your company's name and logo. Perhaps they will sell (or give) you a few for your employees. If not, they will almost certainly help you to order them at a discount.

At one major company, executives above a certain level had special name plaques for their desks. Mary, a senior executive, called to arrange for one for a subordinate about to be promoted. The person on the other end of the line said "And you want a pen set too, right?" It turned out that besides the fancy name plaque, the newly promoted subordinate was entitled to a pen set mounted on a marble base inscribed with her name. Mary ordered one for her subordinate and one for herself as well. No one had told her she was entitled to one, and *her* boss hadn't ordered one for her when *she* had been promoted. She would never have found out if she hadn't called. The same phenomena exists in most corporations—often with things far more important than pen sets.

If calling doesn't work, then try the grapevine. Ask your manager, peers, and subordinates if they know of anyone who can do the work you need. If you need someone to do illustrations, for instance, see if anyone knows of someone who likes to draw cartoons and would be interested in illustrating a booklet. You may find that a level-three accountant tucked away in auditing loves to cartoon and rarely gets the chance. It's always worth a try. If nothing turns up you haven't lost anything; if something does, you are way ahead.

If you want to attend certain types of courses, get exposure by meeting with community leaders, or act in company films, ensure that the areas that coordinate these activities know about your willingness to participate. You'd be surprised how often they use volunteers.

Call Them Before They Call You

There is one circumstance when you should call in the watchdogs— even if you know the word will go up the line and you may get more help and attention—than you want. This is when you have a problem affecting the security of the corporation: cash or equipment disappearing, books that appear to be fixed, employees obviously and dangerously on drugs or mentally ill. You will have to report the problem sometime, or someone will report it for you. It is better, by far, to invite the proper department in and retain some semblance of control than to try to brush the dirt under the carpet. If you invite the auditors in to help you determine whether cash is really going into the pockets of your night-shift employees, the auditors are then reporting to you and to senior management about your problem. This is infinitely preferrable to their reporting only to senior management—with your lack of control a part of the problem they are reporting.

You Don't Need a Bookcase; You Need a Dog Robber

A middle manager in a large research laboratory has one of the best-equipped labs in the company—far better equipment than other managers at his level. His office furniture is almost better than the president's. (He has enough sense not to overstep that line.) His budget is no higher than anyone else's. He has a dog robber on his staff. This term, borrowed from the military, refers to someone who is a specialist at getting the best of what there is and conjuring needed items out of thin air. He confesses to closing his eyes to his dog robber's methods, contenting himself with extracting a firm denial that any actual stealing is taking place every three months or so. Beyond that, with only a slightly guilty conscience, he mentions needed furniture or equipment from time to time and is profuse with his thanks when it appears. He never asks where it came from. And no one has ever appeared in his office to demand the return of stolen property. His new office chair might look suspiciously like one that used to decorate a seldom-used lobby, but no doubt it is only coincidence. He still can't figure out where his man found 90 square feet of plush carpet.

You can't train or develop a dog robber. The best you can do is to try to spot one on your staff. (Or you might find one on someone else's staff and recruit him or her.) Look for the person who—among equals— always has the best furniture. He or she is likely to have lots of equipment and special gadgets. Dog robbers seem to like what they do, finding the best desk in the building is a challenge that cannot be denied. If you think you've found a robber, try dropping a hint that you need a bookcase and don't seem to have the funds for one. If one appears in your office on Monday morning, you're home free.

The Old Boy, Old Girl, and Every Other Kind of Network

Just as you can informally use the expertise of others within your organization (and they, yours), you can extend your reach as far as you can communicate. When you need to learn something new, when you want to find a new supplier, when you want a new job, you can talk to a friend. Then you can talk to a friend of a friend, and then a friend of the friend's friend and so forth until you learn what you need to know. This is called networking. You can develop a network in any area you need help. There are several simple guidelines that make networking easier and more effective:

• Ask for information, not favors.

- If someone can't help you, ask if he or she can refer you to someone who might be able to.

- Don't place unrealistic demands on the time of busy experts.

- Thank everyone who speaks with you (whether he or she actually helped). If you meet over lunch or drinks, you pick up the tab.

- MOST IMPORTANT: Make sure that you share your time and expertise with others who call you.

There are a lot of skills and knowledge all around you. The key is to learn how to tap that knowledge in others and how to share yours with them.

Afterword

There is no substitute for hard work (nor luck, such as being in the right place at the right time) if you want to get ahead in management. But hard work by itself will not do the job. It is hard work applied in the right way in the right places at the right times.

"I'm sorry son, but without a postgraduate degree and at least five years of experience, I can't sell you the Senior Executive briefcase. How about this Up-and-Coming Junior Executive model?"

Whether you work at Ticky, Tacky Industries or Randy's Rodent Rentals, for a government department, or in an entrepreneurial start-up, you have to work with and through people. Some of them will be helpful, some recalcitrant, some friendly, others hostile. But you will have to work with them.

If you follow the techniques suggested in this book, you should find that task a lot easier. Concentrate on establishing and maintaining a relationship with your manager. Work at supporting your boss, but don't hesitate to say no rather than take on jobs that you can't do. Ask for promotions and raises when you deserve them, but ask in the right way. Make sure that *your* ideas get the support they deserve.

Build a staff that will not only do the job but also make you (and them) look good. Manage knowledgably: choose your leadership styles to suit your own temperament and the situation; delegate skillfully; get peak performance from your people. Know what you're doing when you hire so you get the people you really want. Salvage those employees who aren't performing when you can and get rid of them cleanly when you can't, with the minimum of problems for yourself and the company you work for—and the least amount of anxiety.

In sum, do your job—managing—not just to the best of your ability, but intelligently, with planning and understanding of the social mechanics involved.

At the beginning of this book, you put your feet up to relax while you read. Okay. Now it's time to climb out of the hammock or let the fire die in the fireplace and get to work. There's a lot of opportunity out there waiting for people to grab it.

And don't forget to stick this book in a handy drawer. You never know when you may need it.

INDEX